The Gift of Gab

—THE—
GIFT of GAB

65 FUN GAMES & ACTIVITIES
to Help Encourage
SPEECH DEVELOPMENT
in Your Child

FRANCINE DAVIDS,
MS, CCC-SLP

TILLER PRESS

NEW YORK LONDON TORONTO SYDNEY NEW DELHI

TILLER PRESS

An Imprint of Simon & Schuster, Inc.
1230 Avenue of the Americas
New York, NY 10020

First Tiller Press trade paperback edition August 2020

TILLER PRESS and colophon are trademarks of Simon & Schuster, Inc.

For information about special discounts for bulk purchases, please contact Simon & Schuster Special Sales at 1-866-506-1949 or business@simonandschuster.com.

The Simon & Schuster Speakers Bureau can bring authors to your live event. For more information or to book an event, contact the Simon & Schuster Speakers Bureau at 1-866-248-3049 or visit our website at www.simonspeakers.com.

Interior design by Laura Levatino

Manufactured in the United States of America

1 3 5 7 9 10 8 6 4 2

Library of Congress Cataloging-in-Publication Data
Names: Davids, Francine, author.
Title: The gift of gab : 65 fun games & activities to help encourage speech development in your child / by Francine Davids.
Description: First Tiller Press trade paperback edition. | New York : Tiller Press, 2020. | Includes bibliographical references. | Summary: "From a career speech pathologist, a collection of games and activities designed to encourage speech development at every stage, from toddlerhood to the early school years"—Provided by publisher.
Identifiers: LCCN 2020009820 (print) | LCCN 2020009821 (ebook) | ISBN 9781982139858 (paperback) | ISBN 9781982139872 (ebook)
Subjects: LCSH: Children—Language. | Speech—Study and teaching (Early childhood)—Activity programs. | Child development.
Classification: LCC LB1139.L3 D218 2020 (print) | LCC LB1139.L3 (ebook) | DDC 372.6—dc23
LC record available at https://lccn.loc.gov/2020009820
LC ebook record available at https://lccn.loc.gov/2020009821

ISBN 978-1-9821-3985-8
ISBN 978-1-9821-3987-2 (ebook)

To William (Bill) Piazza, who at the age of ninety-one had never forgotten the value of play. This is for you, Dad.

CONTENTS

Introduction:

PUTTING PLAY TO WORK

I spent over thirty years as a speech pathologist in a large elementary school district in a major western state. The students I worked with were enrolled in special-needs preschool classes, general education classes, special education classes, and gifted student classes . . . In other words, the whole spectrum of young humanity came into my classroom. There, I learned the value of play in helping my students accomplish therapeutic goals. And every year I would be reproached by at least one parent, saying, "My son says all they do in your class is play games." As adults, after all, we regard play as a leisure activity, something you do once the real work is done.

But play *is* the work of childhood—as well as the delight. It is how we begin to understand the world we live in, and our place in that world. Play is the way children learn to answer some very important questions, including: Who am I? Who is that person over there? How do I get their attention? How do I get what I want? This process starts at birth, with the very first interactions being between parent and child.

The language that surrounds a baby provides him with the basis for complex thought. The ability to use repetition, imitation, rhythm, and musicality to retain information is a learned linguistic skill. Puzzles encourage the language-based ability to analyze the situation, ask questions, formulate answers, and think abstractly about possible outcomes. All of these skills are taught and reinforced through game play.

This can all be intimidating for a first-time parent, or even a veteran parent with little time to spare. But the good news is, human beings are born communicators. As social beings, we seek out interactions with others to sustain ourselves. The newborn infant knows this instinctively; he has the tools to reach out to his parents, and the parents, in turn, instinctively respond. This book will give parents the skills to build on this natural relationship, optimize their time with their children, and help them develop communication skills that will last a lifetime. And I promise, it will even be fun!

HOW TO USE THIS BOOK

To make the most of the tools offered in this book, you need a basic understanding of what to expect at each stage of your child's development. I want you to avoid the predictable traps of either underestimating your child's abilities or expecting more than your child can give at any stage. Both create stress that can undermine your efforts.

Chapter 1, "Growing Together," presents an overview of what average human development looks like, in terms of motor, language, and social skills. Chapter 2, "Saying It," looks at the development of speech sound production (articulation). Keep in mind that what these chapters describe are guidelines. Some children develop certain skills earlier or later, and still remain well within average range. This information is not meant to create anxiety, but to guide your choice of games and activities your child might enjoy.

These two chapters also include a list of Parent Skills that can help you create a meaningful and open relationship with your child. Some might seem obvious, but their conscious application in the actual moment of learning may take some practice. Try them out—you may be surprised at how effective they are.

Since the topic of this book is games and play, I have included chapter 3, "Toys," which looks at the commercially manufactured toys that are a large part of a child's life. They form the basis of many an adult's fond memories of friends and family. Sometimes expensive, they can represent a major purchasing decision. How do you choose the right toy for your child? How can a toy help your child's language development? What about video games? Are they bad for kids? You will find my thoughts and guidelines about what to look for when purchasing toys.

GAMES FOR EVERY OCCASION

I have provided over sixty games and activities for you to choose from that are appropriate for children ranging in age from infancy to the early elementary school years. Each game description states the Target Skills (the speech, language, motor, and social skills that the game is designed to support), the Materials needed (with several options to spark your creativity whenever possible), and a description of the Object of the Game, so that all players will understand the goal.

These games and activities are selected for their ease, fun, and proven effectiveness. Whenever possible, they have been devised to fit in with a parent's busy life. Many focus on how to bring play into everyday chores and experiences, incorporate play into larger family gatherings, and use games to deepen your relationship with your child. As children mature, the games they prefer become more abstract and fanciful in nature. But don't worry—I have provided everything you need to get started, from games to play with infants and toddlers to creative storytelling and rule-governed card games for school-age kids.

SEVEN CHAPTERS OF GAMES

The games in each chapter are arranged from simplest to most complex, so you can select the game or activity that will allow you and your child the greatest success and enjoyment. The seven chapters are organized as follows:

Nothing Up My Sleeve: These are games and activities played with common household objects, or no materials at all. Easy to play in the spur of the moment.

In the Toy Box: These games and activities maximize speech and language development by using things you find around the house that your child probably already plays with—bath toys, children's books, pots and pans.

I Can Do It Myself!: You can create your own materials together with your child. Introduce your kids to Cootie Catchers and edible play dough. Recipes and patterns are provided. These homemade materials work alone or in combination in a variety of games and activities that support speech and language growth.

Who Goes First?: Avoid those inevitable discussions about fairness with games that teach children language, speech, and social skills they can take to the school playground.

A Full Deck: Card games are fun, portable, and the basis of an infinite number of games and activities. Go to www.simon andschuster.com/books/The-Gift-of-Gab to download a full set of cards you can use with this book. You and your child will soon be creating your own personalized card decks. Great for nonreaders and advanced readers alike.

At Home and On the Road: You can take game play, and language development, with you everywhere you go. These are games to play with your child as you go about the chores of daily life, like grocery shopping and laundry.

Let's Party!: These games and activities allow you to bring game play to larger groups and cross-generational gatherings like birthday parties and family get-togethers—situations that can be challenging for children with developing speech, language, and social skills. The structure of these well-defined games and activities helps ensure that your time together is well spent.

1. GROWING TOGETHER

Being a parent is by turns rewarding, defeating, frustrating, challenging, invigorating, and exhausting. No two siblings are the same; with every child comes a new personality. Thankfully, the early milestones are more consistent. As we explore child development, keep in mind that the "ages" are averages. Some children reach these milestones a bit sooner, some a bit later. Girls are often a bit ahead of boys, especially when it comes to verbal development.

Within each age range I've also included the relevant Parent Skills. Keep in mind that some of these skills will span the whole of childhood; others are stage-specific. Use what works for you and your child. The idea is to enjoy your time together.

THE FIRST INCREDIBLE YEAR

Your infant is a natural wonder. From birth he can communicate with you in several ways. His cries alert you to the presence of hunger, wet diapers, and the need for a cuddle. His coos and snuggles reward your attentions. By three months, his smiles entice you to play. At this point he also begins to vocalize with the seemingly random sounds we call babbling. He soon learns that he can use his own actions to affect his world. He can hold his bottle, grab his toy, hug his puppy, push the peas away and spit them out.

1

By six months he notices that the objects around him seem to appear and disappear as if by magic. At ten months, separation anxiety may become an issue. Most children will utter their first words between nine and eighteen months. By his first birthday, he is likely using his growing collection of one-word phrases to call you and other family members by name, ask for important things he wants, and refuse objects, food, and toys. His sense of self is taking hold. Perhaps he can even crawl or run away from or toward a person or object.

At this stage, play is a one-on-one activity. Even if an adult or other child is involved, the one-year-old will likely prefer to play alone, or with one other person whose role is to offer an object or react to his actions with approval.

IMPORTANT PARENT SKILLS

At this stage you want to "bathe" your child in language. Your most important tools will be Self-Talk, Parallel Talk, and Gestures.

> **Self-Talk:** Narrate your actions and thoughts out loud to your child as you live your life with him. Making breakfast? Describe your choices: "Eggs or oatmeal today? I think oatmeal and fruit will taste good." Feeling confused? Describe your feelings: "I don't know what to do. Should I call Grandma and ask her? I think I will." As you narrate your life, give him a chance to respond. "What do you think? The pink or the blue socks? You think the blue go better with jeans. Okay. I'll wear those today." Self-Talk provides real-time examples of sentence structure, vocabulary, problem solving, thinking skills, and emotional health.

> **Parallel Talk:** The mirror of Self-Talk, Parallel Talk is the description of your child's actions and feelings in real time, as they happen. He makes a face and spits out the peas: "Ugh! You hate peas! Yucky peas!" He eagerly reaches for his bottle: "Mommy, I want juice now. I'm thirsty." His eyes grow sleepy: "You are so tired. Time for a nap." This technique grows with

your child. Once he begins to talk, build on his words and expand his phrases into sentences. If he says, "Cookie," respond with "Want a cookie? A chocolate cookie?" If he says, "Go bye-bye," you say, "Go bye-bye? Want to go to the store?" Bring the expansion back to him to keep the conversation going.

Gestures: Not all communication is verbal. Try pointing to the thing you are talking about. Use vocal inflections and funny voices to illustrate your feelings and his. Listen to music and dance.

THE TERRIFIC TODDLER

Your child is now his own person, with clear preferences and aversions. He finds joy in repetition, and from favorite toys, songs, and cartoon characters. He now knows that objects have permanence, even if he can't see them. He wants to be an active participant in household routines like cleaning up, doing the laundry, and grocery shopping. With a matured concept of object permanence comes the sometimes-pesky concept of possession. Sharing can be a challenge. He begins to note the size, color, and shape of things. He becomes more curious about the outside world. He knows he is a person different from others, and that other people don't always respond to him in the same ways—i.e., Mommy says no to a request for a cookie, but Daddy says yes. The mirror is a great joy. Boy or girl, most toddlers love dressing up and using makeup to change their appearance.

Around age two, he will begin to speak in two- to three-word phrases, such as "My ball" or "Mommy, get it." On average, he will be able to speak more than three hundred words and understand more than one thousand. Now growth begins to happen very quickly. By approximately three years of age, he will begin to use language in expanding ways for many purposes. As his needs become more abstract, so does his language use. He discovers that he can not only ask for what he wants or refuse what he doesn't, he can also talk about what has happened in the past or plan for the future. He can make up his own stories. He discovers that language is not only practical, it's fun.

With the growth of abstract language at about age three, fantasy play begins. Acting out favorite stories, creating his own stories, and taking on different roles become part of play. Patterns take center stage. Rhyming, alliteration, songs, and chants are now fascinating for him. He uses them to poke fun or communicate anger; for example, "Poopy puppy" or "poo-poo head."

As he approaches age four, play becomes more of a group activity, with each participant taking on a different role. Not yet rule-governed, play is fluid and based on imitation of the activities and stories he is most familiar with.

IMPORTANT PARENT SKILLS

Expansion: Now is the time to add Expansion to your language-teaching toolbox. You take your child's simple two- to three-word phrase and add a more adult vocabulary and structure. For example, if he says, "Mommy, cookie," you respond by paraphrasing his statement. "Mommy, give me a cookie? Okay. Let me get it for you." Remember to always respond to the meaning of what he said. Expansion is not a means of correction, but a way to model more sophisticated language use.

This, Then That: Turn everyday activities into participation games. Your toddler has seemingly endless energy and wants to "do" everything he sees others do. This is a good time to introduce the concept of "This, Then That." For example: "First clean up, then have a cookie." "First a bath, then a storybook." "First a storybook, then sleep." This concept also assists with dealing with anticipation. In an age of instant gratification, it is hard for kids to wait. "Hungry? Help make the sandwiches. What goes first? Cheese? Okay, put it on the bread." And "Let's clean up the toys. First one to fill the bucket is first to choose a cookie . . . Go!"

Controlled Choices: Reduce frustration by providing choices for your toddler. Too many items to select from can be overwhelming for both parent and child. Let him choose between two shirts. "This or that" choices are appropriate. Use this technique to build vocabulary (size, shape, color, function) and decision-making values. ("It's raining . . . umbrella or raincoat today?")

Predictability: Reduce anxiety around new experiences by giving your child the powers of prediction, observation, and adaptation. Tell him what you are going to do. Describe for him how you will prepare and what you expect when it happens. ("Let's get ice cream. We'll get our favorite hats and go to Baskin-Robbins. It's hot today. There may be a line, but we will be patient.") Then carry out the plan as you describe again what you are doing. If things go awry, as things sometimes do, describe for him how you can adapt. ("Oh, phooey! They don't have strawberry ice cream. I'm disappointed. I'll get the vanilla. I like vanilla." "Oh no! You dropped the ice cream! No problem, I'll share mine with you.") Then, after the event, discuss the experience with him. How did the plan work? Is he happy with the outcome? ("My ice cream was good. Did you like yours?") This skill builds language in obvious ways, like verb tenses and the concepts of past, present, and future. But it works in more subtle ways as well. He will learn how to handle anticipation through planning, and how to endure disappointment. Your own use of language can influence your child's mastery of his emotional world.

Repetition: At this age, children love watching the same TV shows and movies and hearing the same stories over and over again. It can drive a parent a bit bonkers, but for the child, there is comfort in familiarity. There is also the probability that each time he sees the movie or hears the story, his mind has matured a bit and it may have new meaning for him, or he may notice new details. This makes repetition a valuable way to help him grow in observation, prediction, judgment, and imagination.

Using Repetition with Books: Take advantage of the beautiful and colorful illustrations in children's books. Look for picture books without text. These allow the greatest flexibility in story-telling. If you can't find a suitable picture book, no problem. A book with text can be adapted: At the first reading, cover up the words at the bottom of the page. Examine the pictures together and make up a story based on what you see. Then read the author's story together. There will be surprising differences between your story and the author's. Explore those differences. Then go back and encourage him to tell his own story based on the pictures. Pre-reading skills are no longer passive. They are active, interactive, and imaginative.

Using Repetition with Movies: You can teach your child to be-come an active movie watcher. Watch along with him as often as possible, and observe him as he watches. Is he engaged and interacting with the story? Is he passive and mesmerized? To find out, stop the video at a point where a character does some-thing silly or bad. Ask what he thinks about what is happening, or what he thinks will happen next. Give him ideas on how to understand what is happening. "Why did Pooh go to see Eeyore? I think Eeyore was sad and Pooh is his friend." "Is that character scary? I think he's just silly." See what he has to say. You will often find that the movie he was watching wasn't the same as the one you saw. Is the story different for him than it was earlier? This opens up many conversations for you to share.

THE PRESCHOOL SCHOLAR

Young childhood, ages four to six, is the phase where your "baby" starts to move into the world. He is ready to engage with others on his own terms, with the skills you have taught him safely tucked in his bag of tricks. To make this transition successful, his environment—generally preschool and early elementary school—becomes more rule-driven. Daily routines happen on a defined schedule. Games now have rules to guide play and maintain order. Someone must "go first." Fairness becomes a guiding concept. This sets the stage for conflict, just as his independent friendships grow in importance vis-à-vis family relationships. Maintaining a sense of self within a group, evaluating his own behavior, and adjusting accordingly all become important life skills now.

His physical dexterity has also matured. The games and activities he prefers pose both physical and intellectual challenges. Card games, board games requiring him to move pieces around, computer games requiring timing and prediction, math games, and word games make an appearance right about now.

To see the standard for verbal skills at this age, look on YouTube for videos of four-year-olds telling stories. Notice the growing mastery of narrative. There is a definite story with a series of events, although all grammatic elements are not yet in place. Very little prompting from adults is necessary.

IMPORTANT PARENT SKILLS

Controlled Independence: Parenting now gets a bit trickier. By age four, your toddler has become a young child who is ready to move out into the world with independence, even if *you* are not yet ready! Unfortunately, we don't live in a world where true free-range childhood is a comfortable option for most parents. But we must recognize that a young child needs to learn to navigate the world on his own terms. How do parents manage this balancing act? You can carefully select the environments for your child to experience the beginnings of his independence. Preschool environments are key, and not all are alike. Take your time, talk to friends. Have a tryout day at a school you think may be a good fit. Let him tell you what he thinks. His feeling some control over the choice may reduce his anxiety and give him confidence.

At ages five or six, supervised sports and clubs are exciting options. Look at the published manuals for Cub Scouts or Brownies, and you will see they are designed to encourage group social skills and language skills like memorization and following complex directions.

Continue Learned Parent Skills: Self-Talk, Parallel Talk, Expansion, Building Predictability, and Processing Stories and Events continue and become ever more important. It is time for the communication foundation you put in place the first four years or so of his life to pay off. His increased independence and exposure to the world outside of the family comes with some risk. You need to help him manage that risk. Here is when you learn to ask questions about what happens when you can't be around. Help him with information about upcoming events so that he can make better choices. What will he see? How will he feel? What will he do if he gets lost in a store?

Read Together: Books for this age group are filled with ideas on how to navigate a complex world. Read them together. Do the actions of the characters support your values? If not, why not? Engage on these questions together. When you read aloud, activate your inner actor. Use inflection and gestures. Continue to stop and ask questions. Guess what will happen next. Examine the pictures together for emphasized details. Take the characters of your favorite stories and create new ones together.

MASTERS OF CHILDHOOD

Between the ages of six and eight, your child masters the principles of childhood. These are the golden years. Learning to read and reading to learn are pleasures you can share. Numbers become ideas that can be manipulated, the first steps in mathematical literacy. Game play matures.

The outside world intrudes further on your ability to control your child's experiences, and your role moves closer to that of a guide or coach. Games are a great way to navigate this transition, especially games you create together that build on the firm foundation of the language and social skills you have already provided. Your child now learns that his own actions can influence his successes and failures. He can set goals and can take steps to achieve them. He can enlist groups of people with varying skills to work toward a goal. His abilities extend to independence in school requirements, such as homework completion and project planning. Creativity is the goal at this age. The ability to describe the how and why of his creations will be of increasing value throughout his schooling and on into adult life.

An eight-year-old should be able to relate experiences as a comprehensible series of events. He is very aware that there is a proper way to tell the story, mimicking the inflections he heard when an adult told it to him. Grammatic elements such as verb tense are in place.

IMPORTANT PARENT SKILLS

Setting Limits: At this point, communicating with your child should be a way of life, like eating and breathing. You will exercise the power of setting behavioral boundaries and establishing consequences. Listen to what your child wants to accomplish, and assist him in designing his plan and establishing his own consequences. The object is Self-Discipline. As much as possible, resist the temptation to nag. Your role is to establish household routines that provide opportunities for him to complete tasks such as homework, getting ready for school in the morning, and spending time with friends.

Discipline: If your child's misbehavior did not result in harm to himself or others, I recommend turning the event into a learning experience by providing a "way out." For example: You told him to clean up his room, with the understanding that if he did not do it, he couldn't go to the pizza party on

Friday. He didn't clean up, so no party. Hysteria ensues. But you can give him a way to earn back the privilege. If he cleans his room and empties all the trash cans in the house, then he can go to the party. Now you are not the bad guy, and he learned a lesson.

Scheduling Activities: Some families are challenged to find time together. Busy parents can lead to overscheduled children. While activities can be great for socialization and skill mastery, it's still important at this age for your child to have downtime. Unstructured time is when he has the opportunity to reflect, explore his own interests, play his music, draw his pictures, read for pleasure, see friends, and independently use the life and language processing skills you have gifted to him.

Screens Everywhere: Clearly, pocket electronics, AI, and personal screens will be a part of life from now on. (And who knows what else the future may hold?) You can't fight it, so learn to use the electronics in your life constructively. Share screens when you can. If computer games are his thing but not yours, watch him play and ask him to explain what he is doing. Be a cheerleader. Share a joy of reading? Each of you take a book along as well as a screen when you travel. But other than plane rides and long car trips, strive not to use individual screens while you're together. The goal is connection, whatever the medium.

2. SAYING IT

SPEECH SOUND PRODUCTION, ARTICULATION, AND . . . TWEETY BIRD?

The way we speak and what we say are intertwined. I have found that parents of young children are most often concerned about errors in speech sound production because these errors interfere with their ability to understand what the child wants to say. People outside the family, those least familiar with the child, are likely to point out these errors, implying that the parents need to "do something." But most of these errors, especially in very early speakers, are perfectly natural. Speech development takes years; the child will most likely outgrow them. But how do you tell the difference between age-appropriate articulation patterns and those that warrant more concern? That's exactly what I hope this chapter will help you do.

CARTOONS AND POOR SPEECH EXAMPLES

My favorite cartoons have always been those produced by Warner Bros. in the 1940s and '50s. Maybe it's because Bugs Bunny was the ultimate Brooklynite and I could relate to that. When I grew up, I learned that most of these iconic characters owed their souls to one talented man, Mel Blanc. He was called "the man of a thousand voices." You may never have seen his face, but you are familiar with the approximately four hundred voices he brought to cartoons from the start of the golden age until he left us in 1989. He lent his vocal talents to Bugs Bunny, Porky Pig, Speedy Gonzales, Foghorn Leghorn, Barney (*The Flintstones*) Rubble, and more. He is also the reason I became a speech pathologist.

Mr. Blanc came from an early radio tradition in which the accents and speech of the American community were seen as fair game for comedy. This included the speech of young children. Admittedly, this is an attitude that we no longer buy into in our PC age but is effective in quickly communicating a character. This is a valuable skill when you have to tell a story with only your voice, in less than ten minutes. The way I see it, the genius of Mel Blanc was that he used the speech errors that young children often make to personify his characters. This allowed the children and adults in his audience to immediately identify with the characters. Just by listening to them they knew that Tweety Bird was a baby, Porky Pig was insecure, and Elmer Fudd was immature. Some speech pathologists have written that these cartoon characters are a "bad influence" on the young children who enjoy them because they might imitate these speech patterns. I respectfully disagree. Children exhibited these speech patterns long before radio, sound films, cartoons, and Mr. Blanc were on the scene. It is unlikely that children will acquire these patterns through occasional exposure. Just as with bad behavior, children are far more likely to imitate the speech of the adults they interact with daily. That being said, I do share the concern that children could come to see these patterns as a reason to ridicule or bully the speaker. I firmly believe that with proper adult interaction, children can be taught to understand what they are hearing and respond with humor and compassion.

I bring all of this up for a reason. We are very familiar with these speech patterns. I have used these characters' names in the following examples to give the reader an immediate sound-picture of what these patterns sound like, not to label or shame any parent or child in any way. Over the years the question parents most often ask me is "Should we worry about this?" The answer to that question is not always simple. The next question is always "What can I do?" The best answer to the first question is gather information. The answer to the second question is use game play to foster communication.

A QUICK OVERVIEW OF THE
COMMON SPEECH ERROR TYPES

Speech pathologists, linguists, and elocutionists have developed a catalog of the speech error types most common in young children. These speech errors are present across language groups and cultures. Here are some English examples.

- **Voicing:** Sounds made with no voice are replaced with voiced sounds (e.g., "cat" becomes "gat").
  - I don't associate this error with any cartoon character. Perhaps because it is a subtle error and not as commonly observed as the others.

- **Stopping:** Sounds made with a long airflow are replaced by sounds made with a stopped airflow (e.g., "I taught I taw a putty tat").
  - Okay, you guessed it. Tweety Bird. Very common in early talkers. This pattern should self-correct by age three to four.

- **Final Consonant Deletion:** The ends of words are often missed out (e.g., "cup" = cu').
  - This pattern was not used in cartoons, possibly because it is not as common as some other error patterns or because it would interfere with intelligibility when used in a soundtrack.
  - I found this pattern most often in children with conductive hearing loss from middle ear infections or the presence of middle ear fluid.
    - So, if your child is doing this, talk to your pediatrician about an examination and a hearing screening. It may be nothing, but better to know than to wait.
    - Middle ear infections come and go. If your child has allergies or appears lethargic, even if she doesn't seem ill, you may want to seek a doctor's opinion.

- **Velar Fronting:** Sounds made with the tongue hitting the back of the mouth (e.g., /k/ and /g/) are replaced with sounds made at the front of the mouth (e.g., /t/ and /d/).
  - "Goat" becomes "doat," "cat" becomes "tat."
  - "I taught I taw a putty tat."
  - The quotation most associated with Tweety involves two error processes.
  - Just as with Stopping, this pattern should self-correct by age three to four.

- **Palatal Fronting:** The tongue is moved forward in the mouth so the /sh/ sound becomes a /s/ sound.
  - E.g., "shoe" becomes "sue."

- **Weak Syllable Deletion:** Stressed syllables are deleted from words.
  - E.g., "Elephant" becomes "**efint**" or "**fint**."

- **Assimilation:** Pronunciation of the whole word is influenced by the presence of another sound in the word.
  - E.g., "rabbit" becomes "**babbit**."

- **Consonant Cluster Reduction:** Clusters of consonants in words are reduced by one or more sound.
  - E.g., "trick" becomes "tick," "frown" becomes "fown."

- **Deaffrication:** The sounds /sh/, /ch/, and /dz/ (as in "jelly") are replaced with the fricative sounds /sh/, /s/, /z/ or the stops /t/ or /d/.
  - E.g., "shoe" becomes "too," "chocolate" becomes "socolate," "jelly" becomes "delly."

- **Frontal Lisp:** The sounds /s/ and /z/ are produced with the tongue hitting the upper central incisors or palate, restricting the airflow.
  - E.g., "soap" becomes "**thope**," "zoo" becomes "**thoo**."

- **Gliding:** The /l/ and /r/ sounds are replaced with the /w/ or the /y/ (as in "yellow") sounds.
    - E.g., "rope" becomes "wope," "little" becomes "witto" or "yitto."
    - "That wathkily wabbit."
    - Elmer Fudd exhibits two errors that are common in older, school-age children: Gliding and Frontal Lisp.
    - Both of these errors are later-developing and should self-correct by age seven to eight.

- **Substitution Errors:** These can vary.
    - E.g., the voiceless /th/ sound (as in "bath") is replaced with a /f/ sound (becoming "baff").
        - This pattern is very common in parts of England and in the American South. In those locations it would not be considered an error.
    - The voiced /th/ sound (as in "bathe") is replaced with a /v/ sound and becomes "bave."
    - Substitution errors are most often consistent in nature. The child will "always" substitute the error sound for the target sound, even in blends.
        - E.g., "throat" becomes "froat."

- **Dysfluency:** Most often described as stuttering.
    - If dysfluency persists past age two to three it may be wise to seek a professional evaluation. However, simple sound or syllable repetitions in the speech of very young children are most likely to self-correct as verbal proficiency develops.
        - Resist the urge to tell her to "spit it out" or "slow down."
        - Instead, slow down your own rate of speech. Enunciate clearly and paraphrase her statement.

- Dysfluency can take many forms, from:
  - **Simple sound repetitions** (e.g., "Th-th-th-that's all, folks," made famous by Porky Pig).
  - **Word repetitions** (e.g., "Well, ah say, well, ah say," made famous by Foghorn Leghorn).
  - **Hesitations** (a lot of "um"s and "uh"s).
    - Without naming names, we recently had a very intelligent and gifted speaker in high office who exhibited this type of dysfluency during press conferences.

- **Lateralization:** The sibilant sounds /s/, /z/, /sh/, /ch/, and /j/ (soft /g/ as in "jelly") are produced with the airflow directed out to the right and/or the left, rather than the center of the mouth.
  - This is not a developmental pattern and is not likely to self-correct without professional, structured intervention. Seek advice if this pattern persists past age three.
  - This pattern is sometimes associated with immature swallowing patterns, which can have an adverse effect on the development of dentition and tooth alignment.

REASONABLE EXPECTATIONS, BY AGE

Birth to twelve months: During the first year, don't concern yourself with speech sound production. This is the time to encourage imitation, master your modeling skills, and the give-and-take of conversational interaction. You encourage imitation by first imitating the child. Sound effects like Bugs Bunny's "raspberries" (*Blssstht!*) are always good for a laugh. Plus, they tickle when exploded on a belly button. (Don't judge. You know you have done that.)

Twelve months to three years: Listen for these sounds in words like "Momma," "Papa," "baby," "Daddy," "Mommy," and "teddy": /p/, /b/, /m/, /n/, /t/, /d/. Nicknames are great for practicing these sounds (e.g., Bobby for Robby or Rob).

Almost all children in this age range will exhibit one or two error types. This can be a long and complex learning stage. Errors are to be expected, and the adult ability to model correct production clearly is of greatest importance. It takes time, consistency, patience, and a sense of humor.

Three to four years: Listen for the sounds /p/, /b/, /m/, /n/, /t/, /d/, /k/, /g/, /f/, /s/, /y/, /h/, /w/ to come into play in multiple-syllable words and phrases like "paper towel," "wooden hanger," "funny baboon," and "my grandma." Speech may be unclear to adults who don't know the child well.

The first few error patterns listed above have probably faded by now. The error types Weak Syllable Deletion, Assimilation, Consonant Cluster Reduction, Deaffrication, Gliding, and Substitution may persist but should be fewer in number and less consistent in frequency.

At this point you may notice that errors in speech sound production affect expressive language. For example, omitting final sounds in words can affect verb tense ("follow" versus "followed"). Modeling and patience are called for. If the ability to be understood by family and friends is affected, now is a time you might consider a professional evaluation.

Four to six years: Speech production should be clear and easy to understand by now. The speech sounds /p/, /b/, /m/, /n/, /t/, /d/, /k/, /g/, /f/, /s/, /y/, /h/, /sh/, /ch/, /j/, /z/, /l/, /v/ are mastered. The error patterns Deaffrication, Gliding, and Substitution may persist. If these errors affect intelligibility you may want to seek a professional evaluation to determine if intervention (therapy) is called for, or if the remaining errors are developmental in nature and monitoring is the way to go.

Now is also the time to keep an eye out for spelling errors. When children with substitution errors in speech are encouraged to "sound out" words for spelling, errors are often the result. If this is a problem, you can assist by sounding the word out for her, pairing the letter with the speech sound it represents. Auditory Discrimination, the ability to hear the difference between two similar sounds, is a skill that children with substitution errors sometimes find difficult. (Adult: "It's rabbit, not wabbit." Child: "That's what I said . . . wabbit.") Not to be confused with a hearing loss, auditory discrimination is a matter of perception, not reception. Because most words can still be understood with substitution errors, consider the ultimate goal to be correct spelling. Along with auditory samples, give her written examples so she can work on visual memorization of spelling patterns. Use flash cards if sounding words out is not successful. Memorization is probably the best way to learn spelling in a complex language like English, anyway.

Six to eight years: No specific articulation milestones should remain to be met at this point. Most children can say all of the speech sounds without error. Intelligibility should not be a concern.

If errors persist, and you have not already done so, now is the time to consider getting a qualified professional's opinion regarding evaluation and specialized therapeutic intervention. If no one at your child's school has approached you, contact the school office and make your concerns known.

I know this is a lot of information, but I hope it helps guide your decision about when or if to consult a speech professional. If you remain in doubt, speak to your pediatrician, who can advise on next steps. In the U.S., starting in preschool, an evaluation by a qualified speech pathologist should be available through your local public school district.

In the meantime, resist the temptation to be critical of your child's mispronunciations. Here are Parent Skills you can use to correct without criticism.

PARENT SKILLS: MORE THAN MODELING

Respond to *what* your child is saying, not *how* she says it.
- Remember, "No!," "Say it again," and "That's not right!" are conversation killers.
- Keep the conversation going.

Use Expansion to present more complex speech and language examples.
- Rephrase the statement, slightly, to show you understood what she said.
- Slowly and clearly enunciate the correct sound production with emphasis.
- Give her a moment to say it again, as part of the conversational flow.
  - In other words, don't pressure her to repeat what you said or say it all again.
  - Children are natural mimics. She will likely imitate you in her own way.

Use Auditory Discrimination to improve her ability to hear the difference between correct and incorrect sound productions.
- Make the mistake yourself, and then correct yourself.
- This shows that there is nothing wrong with making a mistake, and provides a correct/incorrect comparison for her to hear.
  - Child: That wabbit ith wunning fath!
  - Adult: Yes, that wabbit, um, rabbit iz running fast.
- Stress the sound(s) you want to model by slightly lengthening the sound production.
  - Child: That wabbit ith wunning fath!
  - Adult: Yes, that rrabbit izz running fasst. Run fast, rabbit!
  - Child: Wun fath, rabbit.

Eye contact is important.
- Face each other whenever possible.
- Maintain a natural level of eye contact.
  - Visual information supports auditory discrimination.

And then, of course, use the games in this book to keep the conversation going!

3. TOYS

Toys have been found in archaeological digs dating to the prehistoric age: doll-like figures and toy-size tools like axes and flints, bows and arrows. If adults used them, kids wanted their own to play with. It's a bit more complicated in the twenty-first century. Toy manufacturers spend millions, if not billions, of dollars every year marketing their wares to parents and children. So how do you sort through the choices to find the toys that will actually help your child with speech and language development?

The best rule of thumb is, in order to learn something, a child must be actively engaged with the toy. If the toy is designed so that the child will passively watch it do its thing, pass it by. Look for toys that require the child to do something to make it work. Instead of a battery-operated toy car, get one that requires a windup key. This adds an element of cause and effect to the play. Instead of a battery-operated "ride 'em" car, get one with bicycle pedals or scooter action. Both are fun and functional, but the second type increases coordination, along with upper- and lower-body strength.

> **Books:** Select books that include some form of interaction to add an element of surprise. Pop-up books, books with textures to explore, windows to open, sound buttons to push: all of these book formats invite even the youngest of children to engage with the written word.

Make your own: If you don't find what you want at your local bookstore or online, make your own. Find small examples of objects with interesting textures (cotton balls, sandpaper, satin fabric, wool yarn, etc.). Cut out two-inch-square examples of each and glue or, better yet, sew them onto four-inch-square pieces of fabric or card stock. (Remember that babies under age three like to put things in their mouths—safety first!) Label each example with its name ("cotton ball") and the texture words you want to highlight ("soft," "fluffy"). Punch holes in the corner of each card and tie them together with a pretty ribbon. Come up with a snappy title for the cover. You're an author!

Use What You Have: For young children (under age four), the immediate environment is what they are most interested in and what they want to explore. Common household objects can inspire limitless imagination. Kitchen pots and pans coupled with a wooden spoon is a great way for a child to learn about sound, rhythm, and music, and cause and effect. Using the dust on the furniture to draw shapes, letters, and pictures is a good way to introduce writing to toddlers as you do the household chores. Besides, it's also a good excuse to give Grandma as to why you skipped the dusting this week.

Toys Don't Have a Gender: Girls like to build spaceships and boys like to play house and cook. My grown daughter still resents that her Lego set was a horse corral and not a spaceship. (In my defense, I maintain that we already had several spaceship kits in my son's collection.) Don't let the toy store marketer control your selection with their color-coded aisles where pink and purple = girl and red, yellow, and blue = boy. I have seen many a girl in a tutu dueling with a lightsaber and many a boy playing happily in a toy kitchen cooking rocks or holding a baby "just like Daddy."

Video Games: By the time you read these words, the video game industry will have changed again. Every holiday season brings another leap in technology or another latest and greatest game console to tempt your kids and empty your pockets. You can't escape it, and to be honest you don't want to. Video games are terrific. You can, however, take a hard look at the marketplace and choose games that offer your family more than idle time in front of yet another screen. Look for games and consoles that accommodate more than one player at a time; that require players to cooperate to obtain their goal; that require the player to solve a puzzle to get to the next level. These formats encourage the players to use and learn new language and social skills. There are games based on historical fact, space exploration, architecture, and city design. If your child has a specific interest, there is a game out there about it that meets one, if not all, of these guidelines.

A PARENT'S GUIDE TO SELECTING TOYS

Here are five types of toys for each age group that your child will really enjoy, but probably won't ask for.

Infants to Toddlers

- Shape sorters
- Newborn–toddler gyms
  - The types where baby lies beneath the hanging "gym" music-makers and must hit them to make the music.
  - Activity cubes that use the same principle. The child must twist or hit the switch to make the noise.
- One- to three-piece wooden puzzles
- Texture books, "baby's first words" picture books
- Ring tower builders

Preschool to Kindergarten

- Wooden blocks
- Interlocking plastic building blocks
- Dress-up costumes/clothes
- Lacing cards
- Play dough, clay

Kindergarten to Grade One
(ages five to six)

- Trace-and-erase chalkboards
- Building sets with gears and pulleys
- Books about kids and school experiences
- Beads and jewelry-making kits
- Simple board games requiring color matching and number concepts

Grades Two to Three
(ages seven to eight)

- Classic Choose Your Own Adventure books
- Model-building or cooking kits that require following multi-step directions to result in a desired outcome
- Physically challenging action games or sports
- Board games that require problem solving
- Creative crafts like sewing, clay modeling, weaving

LET THE GAMES BEGIN!
GAMES, ACTIVITIES, AND ADVICE

*Before we get to the fun part, here are
some valuable pointers for getting
the best from your child.*

- **Accept responses at the level appropriate to your child's abilities.** If your child is not yet verbal, select games that can pivot on pointing or face-making instead.

- **Leave time for some silence.** Adults hate a verbal vacuum, but small children often need time to process what comes next. When you do talk, use the techniques we discussed earlier: Self-Talk, Parallel Talk, and Expansion. Don't pressure the child for a response.

- **Criticism is not allowed.** Nothing stops communication and fun faster than the word "No." Accept your child's responses as they are, and if you want to encourage a different response or point of view, restate or paraphrase what the child said or ask open-ended questions ("I see where you might think that. But I think of it this way." "How would that work?" "What would happen if we did that?"). Discuss, and then continue playing.

- Be a **gracious loser, and a generous winner. Your goal isn't to win the game,** it is to have fun as your child's speech and language skills grow. As an adult you have an unfair advantage. I have found that while children may enjoy a challenge, they want to feel that victory is possible.
  - If you win, let him know he was a worthy opponent. "Boy, oh boy! You were tough to beat today."
  - If he wins, praise him. "That was impressive!"

- You may find that your older child sometimes wants to play a game that you played together when he was much younger. **This doesn't mean he is regressing.** It means that the game brings back pleasant memories of time with you. Go with it. Don't belittle it as a baby game. He'll grow tired of it very quickly, and you will share a laugh together.

- Feel free to **get creative and a little bit silly.**

4. NOTHING UP MY SLEEVE

GAMES AND ACTIVITIES
THAT DO NOT NEED MATERIALS

Lap games, finger games, and rhymes have a long and sometimes colorful history. There are several benefits of finger games, with each game focusing on a slightly different skill set. Infants and other very young children will need assistance in carrying out the choreography of hand gestures at first. Toddlers and older children will enjoy the challenge of perfecting their movements as they sing the songs. These games provide many subtle benefits in addition to language development, including pleasurable social interaction, the acceptance of physical comfort, and an introduction to gestural language.

1. Rub-a-Dub-Dub

Target Skills: Body Part Vocabulary, Right/Left Discrimination, Musicality, Self-Identity

Materials: You can play this game with just your baby, a washcloth, and some water, but for our example we'll use: Baby bathtub (or other small bathing tub), baby bath seat or slant sponge, baby bubble bath, baby shampoo, baby lotion, a soft towel. *Optional*: Diaper supplies, waterproof baby doll.

Note: Safety is always the first consideration. Never leave your child unattended around water, even for a moment. There are many baby bathtubs and bath seats on the market at varying price points, but nothing takes the place of an alert adult.

Object of the Game: As your child enjoys her bath, she will learn to identify her facial features and body parts.

Step One: Prepare the bath.
- Place baby in a comfortable seat where she can see you as you work. Remember to use your Self-Talk skills as you prepare the bath. This is a moment for happy anticipation.
- Be sure that you are in a comfortable position, too. You don't want to rush bath time.
- The water should be no deeper than to cover the baby's bum when she is sitting up, a maximum of a few inches. Add the bubble bath as you add the water.
- Keep the water at a lukewarm temperature. Test the water with your hand or elbow before placing baby in the bath. If your skin turns red from too much heat, it is too warm for your child.
- Place your child in the bath. Use a support such as a bath seat or slant sponge to keep her head safely out of the water.
- Time to soap up. Start at the top by gently washing her hair, face, then arms, torso, legs, and finally, the bum. The idea is to clean the dirtiest part of her body (the dreaded diaper area) last.

Step Two: As you gently wash your child, sing or chant a little song that identifies her facial features and body parts. Bubbles are great for emphasizing these features as you go. It can be any tune you like. Here is an example:

(To the tune of "Mary Had a Little Lamb")

> *(Baby) had a little nose, little nose, little nose*
> *(Baby) had a little nose,*
> *and (Mommy/Daddy) washed it up*

Step Three: Repeat for each body part (toes, feet, ears, neck, etc.) as you wash. If you don't feel comfortable singing, that's okay. Keep up your fancy patter by generally following this sequence:
- Tell her what you are going to do.
  - *"I am going to wash your nose. Here I come!"*
- Tell her what you are doing.
  - *"I like washing your nose, it's so cute."*
- Tell her what you did.
  - *"Okay. Your nose is clean!"*
- Ask her what the next part to wash should be or tell her what you will wash next.
  - *"Should we wash your right foot next? Let's start with your toes!"*

Step Four: For children who can sit up on their own in the bath. If you have a waterproof doll available, you can demonstrate as you go by showing her what you will do. Encourage her to wash the "baby," too. This is a good time to emphasize words like "gently," "clean," and "love."

Step Five: Continue to narrate what you are doing as you towel-dry, lotion, and dress her. Repetition of the vocabulary is key.

2. Classic Peekaboo!

Every baby's favorite game since there have been babies. There is a reason for that. It's *fun* for both baby and adult. You can get as goofy as you'd like. But there's also a purpose. As a sophisticated parent you now know that your infant is learning from this seemingly simple activity.

Target Skills: Object Permanence, Predicting and Anticipating the Actions of Others

Materials: Hands to hide your face. *Optional*: Cloth or towel, blanket, piece of paper, or book.

Object of the Game: The child will giggle in anticipation of the adult's disappearance and reappearance.

Step One: Take care of your baby's physical needs first. Make sure she is fed, rested, and dry. If your baby is distracted by hunger or discomfort, she will not enjoy playtime. She may even cry.

Step Two: Is baby paying attention to you? Sit her in a bouncy chair, prop her up on your knee facing you, any position in which she is safe, comfortable, and able to see you easily.

Step Three: Look for her extended eye contact and little wiggle of excitement when you talk to her. That's how she signals she is ready to engage. Eye contact is key to a good game of peekaboo. Start by making a funny face, singing in a funny voice, or making surprising noises. Farting noises are universally entertaining and never lose their ability to delight (ask any twelve-year-old boy). Just like any good entertainer, watch for your baby's reaction. She'll let you know what's working for her and what isn't.

Step Four: Start by covering your face with your hands. After baby has learned the delight of peekaboo, you can move to "hiding" behind a cloth or towel. But initially, your hands will be more comforting to her. Until she masters object permanence, you are not hiding . . . you have mysteriously disappeared!

Step Five: Keep talking to your baby as you "hide" to keep yourself in her presence. "Where am I?"

Step Six: "Reappear" by taking your hands away from your face. "Peekaboo! Here I am!" Make a different face or have a different expression each time you "reveal."

Never be "gone" for more than a second. The goal is delightful surprise, not anxiety about your return.

Step Seven: Carefully watch your baby's reaction. A turned head, distressed quivering lip, or wrinkled forehead are probably indications that she is a bit overwhelmed. Hug and kiss her, reassure her, and try again another time.

Step Eight: Once your baby has come to enjoy peekaboo, you can mix things up a bit. Hide behind a towel, blanket, piece of paper, or a book.

Step Nine: Cool down. Don't abruptly stop any game your baby is enjoying to play. If you must get to another chore or make an important phone call, a gentle hug and a snuggle will end the game well. Then provide her with a transition activity. This could be a favorite fluffy toy, a bottle (if it's mealtime), or a music-playing mobile. Baby will learn that the end of playtime is not a rejection.

3. Where's Your Nose?

Target Skills: Body Part Vocabulary, Right/Left Discrimination, Following Simple Directions, Self-Identity

Materials: A lap, hands, a comfortable chair

Object of the Game: Your child will identify her facial features and body parts.

Step One: Seat baby comfortably where she can easily see you.

Step Two: You can introduce this game to your child at any age, although usually a child won't actively participate until she is four to six months old.

Step Three: Use an interesting voice. Babies seem to attend to a slightly higher-pitched voice.
- Ask, "Where's your nose?"
- Then point and say, "There it is!"

Step Four: Repeat the nose a few times. Then have her identify your nose.
- If you need to help her, take her hand and touch your nose.
- Make a little sound effect (*Beep!*) when you touch her nose or she touches yours.

Step Five: Play the game with other features and body parts: eyes, ears, neck, belly button.
- A gentle kiss, tickle, or nuzzle usually results in giggles.

4. This Little Piggy

Most appropriate for infants and small children, "This Little Piggy" has a long history. According to Wikipedia, it was in 1728 that the first line of this rhyme appeared in a medley called "The Nurses Song." It wasn't until 1760 that the full rhyme appeared in *The Famous Tommy Thumb's Little Story-Book*. A true classic.

Target Skills: Memory, Prediction and Anticipation of the Actions of Others, Body Awareness, Vocabulary

Materials: Hands and baby's feet, and a lap, baby seat, or dressing mat

Object of the Game: The child will learn the rhyme along with vocabulary.

Step One: Assure that your child is firmly seated in your lap, in a baby seat, or on a dressing mat, as squealy-squiggling-giggling is a likely accompaniment to this rhyme. This is a marvelous post-bath and dressing game. Make it part of your routine.

Step Two: With a light and tickly touch, gently wiggle each toe starting with the big toe on her foot. Right or left will do. When you get to the last line ("All the way home!"), run your fingers up her body, tickling gently all the way up to her neck.

Step Three: Just in case you don't know it . . .

This little piggy went to market,	Wiggle the big toe
This little piggy stayed home,	Wiggle the next toe
This little piggy had roast beef,	Wiggle the middle toe
This little piggy had none,	Wiggle the next toe
And this little piggy cried "Wee wee wee"	Wiggle the pinky toe
All the way home.	Tickle-tickle up to baby's neck
	Optional: Hugs and Kisses

5. Where Is Thumbkin?

Some people think this rhyme started on a 1980s children's TV show that shall remain nameless in this book. I call FALSE on this one. I know I played this with children long before that purple dinosaur ever came on the scene. The song "Frere Jacques," which provides the tune for this game, is French. It dates approximately from the 1600s. The first published appearance of "Frere Jacques" is from around 1780 in a book titled *Recueil de Timbres de Vaudevilles*. You and your child will continue a historic tradition as you sing.

Target Skills: Object Permanence, Memory Vocabulary, Right/Left Discrimination, Reciprocal and Polite Greetings

Materials: Hands

Object of the Game: The child will sing the rhyme as she carries out the hand choreography.

Step One: Comfortably seat yourself and your child opposite each other, with room for each of you to move your arms about.

Step Two: Where Is Thumbkin? is a simple game, but has multi-step choreography: Sing the words to the tune of "Frere Jacques."

1. Start the song with both hands behind your back.
    "Where is Thumbkin? Where is Thumbkin?"

     2. Bring right hand to front, with thumb up.
    "Here I am."

3. Bring left hand to front, with thumb up.
    "Here I am."

4. Wiggle left thumb as if it is talking to right thumb.
    "How are you today, sir?"

     5. Wiggle right thumb as if it is talking to left thumb.
    "Very well, I thank you."

6. With an exaggerated arm movement around your body, hide your left hand behind your back.
    "Run away."

     7. With an exaggerated arm movement around your body, hide your right hand behind your back.
    "Run away."

Steps Two through Six: The song and choreography repeat with each successive finger identified as follows.

Step Two: Where is Pointer? Index finger

Step Three: Where is Middleman? Middle finger (this finger may be tricky; keep the choreography identical with the other fingers)

Step Four: Where is Ringman? The fourth finger, or "ring finger"

Step Five: Where is Pinky? The little finger

Step Six: Where is the family? Bring hand to front, with all fingers showing.

The words of the song are the same, except "I thank you" changes to "we thank you."

6. Itsy-Bitsy Spider

There was a bit of disagreement in my research about the origins of this song. One source said that it dates to 1920, another dates it to 1910. Both agree that it began as a camp song for adults in the publication *Camp and Camino in Lower California*, with slightly more adult lyrics. It was first published as a children's rhyme in 1948. So now you know.

Target Skills: Sequencing, Prepositions, Vocabulary, Memory, Fine and Gross Motor

Materials: Hands and fingers

Object of the Game: The child will sing the rhyme as she carries out the hand choreography.

Step One: The child can be held on your lap, to make it easier for you to assist with the arm and hand motions, or seated in front of you so that she can imitate your motions as you sing the song together.

Step Two: "Itsy-Bitsy Spider" is a one-verse song with multiple gestures:

Alternate placing the thumb of one hand to the index finger of the other hand (right to left, left to right) as you sing:
> *The itsy-bitsy spider went up the water spout.*

As you bring your arms down, wiggle your fingers to simulate rain as you sing:
> *Down came the rain,*

With palms facing the floor, crisscross your arms across your body:
> *and washed the spider out.*

Join your hands and form a circle with your arms and raise your hands above your head:
> *Out came the sun,*

Lower your arms in a sweeping circular motion:
> *and dried up all the rain,*

Alternate placing the thumb of one hand to the index finger of the other hand (right to left, left to right):
> *and the itsy-bitsy spider went up the spout again.*

7. The Wheels on the Bus

"The Wheels on the Bus" is the most recent addition to our selection of popular children's songs. Written by an American woman named Verna Hills (1898–1990), it was published in 1939 and gained popularity as the automobile became more common. I have modified it a bit for my own version that I like to use with preschool children. When you get to the end, you will see why.

Target Skills: Gestural Sequencing, Associations, Prepositions, Memory, Fine and Gross Motor

Materials: Your own body

Object of the Game: The child will sing the rhyme as she carries out the hand choreography.

Step One: Comfortably stand opposite your child, or in a circle if there are more children, so that you can all see each other. Be sure that you all have enough room to carry out the game's choreography, which sometimes requires jumping and twirling.

Step Two: First verse. Cross both arms forward in front of you. In a circular motion, move your arms around each other continuously as you sing:

> *The wheels on the bus go round and round,*
> *Round and round, round and round.*
> *The wheels on the bus go round and round,*

Move arms up and over your head in a circle in front of you as you sing:

> *All day long.*

Step Three: Second verse. Tap your nose continuously as you sing:

> *The horn on the bus goes "toot toot toot,"*
> *"Toot toot toot, toot toot toot."*
> *The horn on the bus goes "toot toot toot,"*

Move arms up and over your head in a circle in front of you as you sing:

> *All day long.*

Step Four: Third verse. Continuously move your bent arms back and forth in front of your body, like windshield wipers, as you sing:

> *The wipers on the bus go "swish swish swish,"*
> *"Swish swish swish, swish swish swish."*
> *The wipers on the bus go "swish swish swish,"*

Move arms up and over your head in a circle in front of you as you sing:

> *All day long.*

Step Five: Verse four. Continuously bend your knees and then straighten them to make an up-and-down motion. Children will want to jump, and that's okay.

> *The people on the bus go up and down,*
> *Up and down, up and down.*
> *The people on the bus go up and down,*

Stand straight up and move arms up and over your head in a circle in front of you as you sing:

> *All day long.*

Step Six: Verse five. Hold your hands in front of your eyes and continuously open and close your hands as you sing:

> *The lights on the bus go blink blink blink,*
> *Blink blink blink, blink blink blink.*
> *The lights on the bus go blink blink blink,*

Move arms up and over your head in a circle in front of you as you sing:

> *All day long.*

Step Seven: Verse six. Whisper as you tilt your head and hold your hands together next to your cheek, like a pillow, as you sing:

> *The babies on the bus all go to sleep,*

Sing slowly as you continue to whisper and hold your hands next to your face. Flutter your eyes, sleepily.

> *Go to sleep, go to sleep.*

Sing even more slowly. Sink to the floor.

> *The babies on the bus all go to sleep,*

Curl up on the floor and take a sleeping pose.

> *All night long.*

Step Eight: When everyone is quiet, jump up and cheer, "Hooray!" You finished the song!

8. Clap Hands, Clap Hands

Hand-clapping games are international in popularity. Usually there are two people playing together, doing a series of clap patterns with their own and/or each other's hands while singing simple rhymes.

Target Skills: Syllabication and Rhythmic Movement, Memory, Patterns, Speech Sound Pronunciation

Materials: Hands. *Optional*: A drum and drumsticks, a pot and a wooden spoon. Clap Hands is usually a two-player game.

Object of the Game: Using motor patterning as a support, the child will memorize short rhythmic patterns and songs.

Step One: Player One claps her hands along with the rhythm of the sentence, phrase, poem, or song (examples below).

Step Two: Player Two repeats the rhyme and rhythmic clapping response.

Sample chants:

Pat-a-Cake

Pat-a-cake, Pat-a-cake
Baker's man
Bake me a cake as fast as you can
Pat it and prick it
And mark it with B
And there will be plenty for baby and me!

Peas Porridge Hot

Peas porridge hot, peas porridge cold,
Peas porridge in the pot, nine days old;
Some like it hot, some like it cold,
Some like it in the pot, nine days old.

9. Hand Jives

Hand jives have proven popular with older children (ages six and up) who enjoy the challenge of rapidly carrying out the sometimes-complicated hand-movement choreography as they sing songs that require some on-the-spot thinking. These games can be played with as few as two people or in much larger groups. When seated in a circle this can be a very challenging activity (described below). When standing in two opposing lines, this becomes a performance art as players synchronize their movements as they sing along. There are many rhymes and songs to choose from. Every human culture that has children has a treasure trove of these games to investigate. That is part of the fun.

Target Skills: Syllabication, Vocabulary, Right/Left Discrimination, Memory, Rhythm, Speech Sound Production, Cooperation

Materials: Hands

Object of the Game: All players cooperate to keep the hand jive going without error for as long as the song lasts.

Variations: There are as many variations of hand jive games as there are groups of children to play them. Here are two to get you started.

Jive One

Step One: Two players sit or stand opposite each other, singing or chanting a song together (see page 44). They clap their hands in the following pattern as they chant each syllable.

Step Two: Basic Clap Pattern for Two Player Jive

1. Players One and Two clap their own hands together.
2. Players One and Two clap hands with each other, directly across from each other.
   - Player One's right hand to Player Two's left.
   - Player One's left hand to Player Two's right.
3. Players One and Two clap their own hands together.
4. Players One and Two clap one hand with each other, diagonally.
   - Player One's right hand to Player Two's right.
5. Players One and Two clap their own hands together.
6. Players One and Two clap one hand with each other, diagonally.
   - Player One's left hand to Player Two's left.
7. Clap steps are typically repeated when syllables or words are repeated in the chant.
8. Repeat pattern.

Jive Two

Step One: Three or more players are seated or standing in a circle, singing or chanting a song together (see page 44). They clap their hands in the following pattern as they chant each syllable.

Step Two: Basic Clap Pattern for Three Player Jive

1. All players clap their own hands together.
2. All players clap their hands to the players on either side.
   - Right hand to the left hand of the player on their right side.
   - Left hand to the right hand of the player on their left side.
3. All players clap their own hands together.

4. All players clap their hands to the players' hands on either side, crossing their arms across their body, right arm in front.
   - Left hand to the right hand of the player on their right side.
   - Right hand to the left hand of the player on their left side.
5. All players clap their own hands together.
6. All players clap their hands to the players' hands on either side, crossing their arms across their body, left arm in front.
   - Left hand to the right hand of the player on their right side.
   - Right hand to the left hand of the player on their left side.
7. All players clap their own hands together.
8. Clap steps are typically repeated when syllables or words are repeated in the chant.
9. Repeat pattern.

Chants and songs dictate the speed and rhythm of the hand jive, with gestures repeated when words or phrases are repeated. The more complex the song, the greater the challenge. Here is a fan favorite:

Miss Mary Mack

Miss Mary Mack, Mack, Mack
All dressed in black, black, black
With silver buttons, buttons, buttons
All down her back, back, back
   (or *Up and down her back, back, back*).
She asked her mother, mother, mother
for fifty (or *fifteen*) *cents, cents, cents*

To see the elephants, elephants, elephants
    (or *hippos* or *cows*)
Jump the fence, fence, fence.
They jumped (or *flew*) so high, high, high
They reached the sky, sky, sky
And didn't come (or *never came*) back, back, back
Till the Fourth of July, -ly, -ly.
She asked her mother, mother, mother
For five cents more, more, more
To see the elephants, elephants, elephants
Jump the door, door, door.
They jumped to the flow, flow, flow
They stubbed their toe, toe, toe
And that was the end, end, end
Of the elephant show, show, show.

5. IN THE TOY BOX

GAMES THAT USE WHAT YOU ALREADY HAVE

As we discovered in chapter 3, "Toys," toy collections represent an investment of time and money on the part of parents and grandparents. Many of these toys go neglected and unused after the first few hours of play. (In my family, we call that "a five-minute ho-ho.") How do you use these toys to grow your child's speech and language? When you look at a toy, look past the intention of the toy designer and make it work for your child's needs in a new way. Here are some suggestions:

10. Rolling (Soft Toss) Catch

One of those games played throughout history, all over the world in every culture and language group, is catch. The participants throw, toss, or roll a ball or another object to each other, trying not to drop it. A simple game of catch can teach a very young child language skills like Following Directions and social skills such as the Value of Persistence.

Target Skills: Following Directions, Vocabulary (Prerequisite skill: Child should be able to sit up either independently or with minimal assistance.)

Materials: Vary objects as per your child's preference: balls, rag dolls, small stuffed toys

Note: Be aware of safety issues in selecting objects for play. Avoid sharp or hard objects and stuffed toys with loose parts like button eyes.

Object of the Game: To encourage reciprocal play by tossing or rolling the toy between you and your child for multiple turns. To encourage the adult to use the Self-Talk and Parallel Talk techniques.

Step One: Identify a safe, suitable toy that interests your child. The child must indicate that he "wants" the toy, to encourage him to grab for it when it is rolled toward him. Let him play with the toy for a while, describing the toy to him, and sharing in his enjoyment.

Step Two: Once he has enjoyed the toy and is beginning to lose interest in holding it, gently take the toy and entice him with it. Say something such as "Want this back?" or "Want it?"

Step Three: Roll, gently toss, or give it to him, saying, "Here it comes!" *before* he can become upset. Remember, this is play.

Step Four: Once he has gained hold of the toy (you may need to assist him in getting hold of it), cheer for him. "Yay, you got it!"

Step Five: Encourage reciprocity. Say, "Your turn! Send it to me!" You may have to assist him in rolling, tossing, or even just handing the toy to you.

Step Six: Reward him with a small cheer when he has completed Step Five.

Step Seven: Repeat the game from Step Three. Continue until the child signals he is tired of the game.

Variations: The game can be played with multiple children sitting in a circle or spread out over a playing field. Throwing or rolling can take an agreed-upon pattern or occur randomly to an unsuspecting partner. Random play keeps players vigilant while playing.

You can also define the duration of play using music.

11. Beat It!

Target Skills: Patterns, Auditory Discrimination, Imitating Rhythm, Sequencing, Musicality

Materials: Toy xylophone, whistle, jingle bells, pots and pans, wooden spoons, plastic bowls and tubs, wooden boxes. A variety of things that can be struck to make a variety of noises. Remember: Safety first!

Object of the Game: The child will repeat the sound pattern by hitting an array of objects in imitation of the adult's pattern.

Step One: Bring out that toy xylophone, whistles, bells, and those pots, pans, boxes, plastic bowls, and tubs that you are comfortable having your child playing with. We all have some of these in closets or cabinets. Wooden spoons are good to use as drumsticks, but you may have some plastic cooking utensils that you can use. Every combination of stick and drum will produce a different sound. Try to get some high and some low sounds in the mix.

Step Two: Let him explore the objects independently. Just moving the pots and pans around on the floor will produce a symphony of sounds.

Step Three: Begin by imitating him. Every time he hits a pan with the spoon, you do it. That will get his attention. You will know that he understands this part of the game when he looks at you, hits the pot, and then waits for you to imitate him.

Step Four: Once he signals that he understands the imitation part of the game, it's time for you to take the lead. Look him directly in the eye, hit the pot two times, and then wait for him to imitate you. You can verbally cue him ("You do it"). If he appears a bit confused, hit the pot again and then take his hand and help him to do it.

Step Five: Vary the sound pattern by using the different noise-makers, "sticks," and pots you have gathered. You might start your own family band with an eclectic rhythm section.

12. What Does the Cat Say?

Children have a natural curiosity about animals. This game uses sound to encourage a child to investigate his world.

Target Skills: Sound Discrimination, Associations, Vocabulary, Imitation, Categorization, Generalization of Concepts

Materials: Small animal figures, or an illustrated book of animals

Object of the Game: To pair the animal with the sound it makes and imitate that sound in preparation for the imitation skills necessary for speech development.

Step One: Introduce the animals and demonstrate the sounds they make. This will be interesting to newborn babies as well as preschool-age children. A child's understanding and ability to participate in the game will change as he matures. Here are a few to get you started:

- Dog: *woof woof*
- Cat: *meow*
- Fish: *glub glub*
- Bird: *tweet tweet*
- Cow: *moo*
- Rooster: *cock-a-doodle-doo*
- Pig: *oink oink*
- Lion: *ROAR!*
- Peacock: *screech*

Step Two: Vary the pictures, toys, and illustrated books you use when playing the game. This helps to introduce the general concept of *dog* or *cat*, etc., not a specific dog or cat.

Step Three: Ask the question in two ways:

- What does a rooster say?
- Who says cock-a-doodle-doo?

Step Four: In infants, watch the direction of their gaze. If he is attending, celebrate his attention! If he points to an animal, terrific!

Step Five: Encourage him to make the animal noises along with you.

Step Six: Vary the game so that he makes the noise and you guess the animal.

13. What Made That Noise?

Target Skills: Sound Discrimination, Associations, Vocabulary, Imitation, Categorization, Generalization of Concepts, Sound Localization

Materials: A minimum of two toys, such as a rattle, a squeaky toy, a whistle, or any toy or object that can make a distinctive sound. A blanket, towel, large book, or scarf, or anything you can hide two to three objects behind. Be sure to keep safety in mind as to moving parts, small parts, etc. Very young children should never be left unsupervised when around toys.

Object of the Game: The child will identify an object from the sound it makes.

Step One: For very young children, under one year old, make sure they are comfortable and safe, and in a position where they can see the toys. A position in an infant carrier or seat may work well, as long as both of his hands are free to hold the toy and explore the sounds.

Step Two: Gather at least two noisemaking toys. They should be interesting to look at, and colorful, if possible (something that will gain your child's attention). For our example we will choose a rattle and a squeaky bath time rubber ducky.

Step Three: Individually introduce the toys to your child. Since you have selected toys that are safe for him, encourage him to hold and explore the toy and how it makes noise. Remember your Self-Talk and Parallel Talk skills. Describe the toy to him as you play together. The way it feels, its color, its sound; everything you can tell him is important.

Use the name of the toy frequently in your description. For example:

- The rubber ducky is smooth, yellow, with an orange beak. It makes a *squeak* when you squeeze it. It smells like bubble bath!
  - Let him hold it. If he can't, help him grip it in his hand.
  - Encourage him to squeeze it to make the squeak.
- The rattle is shiny and has bumps on it. It is silver. It makes a sound when you shake it. The harder you shake it, the louder the rattle.
  - Let him hold it. If he can't, help him grip it in his hand.
  - Encourage him to shake it to make it rattle.

Step Four: Once you are confident that he knows the toys and the sounds they make, try to identify the one he prefers. For our example it will be the bath time rubber ducky.

Step Five: Take both toys and place them next to each other in front of him. Let him see them both. Give them a squeeze and a rattle so he can hear them again. Then cover them with the towel.

Step Six: Reach under the towel and squeeze the rubber ducky. Act surprised. "What was that? What made that noise?"

Step Seven: Remove the towel. Ask again, "What made that noise?" If he is too young to reach for the toy, watch his eyes. Then take the toy he is looking at and ask, "Was it this?"

Step Eight: Squeeze the ducky or shake the rattle, whichever one he looks at or reaches for.

- If he reaches for the correct one, celebrate. "Yay! You are right, it was the ducky."

• If he is incorrect, explore the sounds again. "No, that's not it. That was a rattle noise. We heard a squeak. Was it the ducky?" Squeeze and squeak. "Yay, we found it! It was the ducky."

Step Nine: Repeat as many times as your child will enjoy.

14. Can You Feel It!

Target Skills: Descriptive Vocabulary, Object Labels and Function, Compare/Contrast, Sensory Discrimination

Materials: Pillowcase or blindfold (an airline eye mask works here). Pairs of household objects that can be held in your hand (bath sponges, damp and dry; rubber balls; plastic and metal spoons; paper or cloth napkins; socks; baby shoes; etc.). Favorite hand-size toys, like a baby doll, a ball, or a binky. Keep safety in mind in your selection. Remember: Toddlers love to explore with their taste buds!

Object of the Game: The child will identify objects using touch alone.

Step One: Gather your materials. When introducing this game to a very young child, limit your selection to three or four pairs of objects with widely differing shapes, textures, and functions. For our example we choose:
• A pair of children's socks
• A pair of plastic spoons
• A pair of soft, clean bath sponges (very squishy)
• A pair of square wooden blocks

Step Two: Introduce the objects. Name them, demonstrate to each other the ways they are used, explore their textures, sizes, and shapes. Use at least two descriptive terms for each object. Remember to use terms for qualities you can feel, not see. Colors and design patterns are not important for this game.

- A pair of children's socks
  - Soft, comfy, worn on your feet, small
- A pair of plastic spoons
  - Smooth, hard, long, then round at the end, use it to eat cereal or soup
- A pair of soft, clean bath sponges
  - Squishy, wet, round or rectangular, bumpy, used to clean your body when you take a bath
- A pair of square wooden blocks
  - Hard, medium-size, square, smooth, have edges, used when you build a tower

Step Three: When you have fully explored all of the objects, explain that you are going to play a game. Your child can't peek! Bring out the eye mask or the pillowcase, whichever one your child will enjoy most. For our example we will use the pillowcase.

- Ask him to close his eyes tight, don't peek!
- Explain that you will place one object in the pillowcase. He will reach in and just by feeling the object he will tell you what it is.
- Place one object in the pillowcase (for our example, a bath sponge).
- If your child is very young, he may need some visual clues. You can place one of each pair of the four objects (bath sponge, sock, spoon, wooden block) on the table for him to see.

Step Four: Ask him to open his eyes (he sees the four objects on the table) and reach into the pillowcase. Encourage him to feel the object and tell you what he feels. You have already given him the words in Step One.

- If he has difficulty in describing the object, ask him some questions.
  - Is it hard or soft?
  - Is it wet or dry?
  - Is it bumpy or smooth?
  - Is it round or square?

Step Five: When he has explored the object, he is ready to guess what is in the pillowcase.

- Remember to celebrate when he is correct ("Yay!").
- Then use it or pantomime its use. Talk about the function. Repeat with another object.

If he is not correct, make a big show of looking in the pillowcase. Pause and say, "No, that's not it." Take the object he guessed away from the table. Let him explore the object in the pillowcase again. Let him feel the objects on the table to compare.

- Does it feel hard like this one? (Point to the spoon.)
- Does it feel square like this one? (Point to the block.)

Step Six: If he does not recognize the object in the pillowcase, consider removing all but two very different objects from view, for example the plastic spoon and the sponge. Let him feel the hidden object and the objects on the table at the same time. That should lead him to the correct answer.

- Remember to celebrate when he gets it right ("Yay!").
- Pretend to use it. Let him pretend.

Step Seven: When he has mastered the rules of the game, play the game with up to five objects, removing the visual cues. Reverse roles and let him select and hide the object for you to guess.

- To make it even more challenging, take turns finding

an object to hide in the pillowcase from around the house. Place it in the pillowcase without discussing it first.

- Then, from tactile cues only, the child must describe the object and guess what it is.

6. I CAN DO IT MYSELF!

GAMES AND ACTIVITIES
USING HOMEMADE MATERIALS

These games and activities allow you and your child to make your own materials and use them to have fun playing your own personalized family games. Children love to make things. These activities render complex language skills like following multistep directions accessible to young children. The child gains the added benefit of being able to immediately see and use the fruits of her efforts.

15. Shake, Rattle, and Roll

Bits and bobs around the house can be used to create unique toys for any age. Safety is always the first consideration, of course. Even with manufactured toys, parental supervision is a must. But don't let that stop you. You can make something unique to suit your child's interest.

Target Skills: Auditory Stimulation, Localizing to Sound, Gross Motor Skills

Materials: Empty two-liter plastic bottle(s) with screw-on tops, packing tape or waterproof masking tape, waterproof superglue, small objects (rice, colorful buttons, plastic building blocks, sparkles, jingle bells). *Optional*: Jell-O mix, food coloring, liquid dish soap, vegetable oil, tap water.

Object of the Game: To follow the sound and "get" the object.

Step One: Gather your materials. Remember: The first consideration is safety. Be extra sure that the bottle is filled with nontoxic items and that the top is firmly and permanently fastened when you are done.
- Fill empty bottles with interesting things:
  - Rice, buttons, plastic blocks, jingle bells, sparkles.
  - Things that will make a noise or catch the light in the bottle when you shake it.
- *Optional*: Add visual interest with a medium that the objects can float in.
  - Fill only halfway to allow movement.
  - Use Jell-O mix and water.
  - Use water mixed with liquid soap, food coloring, or vegetable oil.

Step Two: Firmly and permanently secure the bottle cap back onto the bottle.
- Tightly fasten the top with superglue.
- Use packing tape or waterproof masking tape over the cap and the bottle top to be extra sure nothing will open or leak.

Step Three: Always supervise your child's play. Kids who crawl or toddle love to explore with their taste buds. You want to be sure your child can't chew through the bottle.

Step Four: Once you are satisfied with the look and safety of your creation, enjoy it with your child.

- Shake it, letting the objects float and move to catch her attention.
- Listen with her to the sounds it makes when you shake it.
- Describe it to her. (Use your Parallel, Self-Talk, and Expansion skills.)

Step Five: Once you have explored the toy together, roll the bottle across the floor away from her.
- Crawlers and toddlers will enjoy going to "Get it!"
- Make a few different toys for her to explore.

16. DIY Cards

One fun way to personalize card games for your child is by making your own cards. To find downloadable templates you can use to make all kinds of cards and game boards out of poster paper or cardboard, please visit simonandschuster.com/books/The-Gift-of-Gab, and scroll to "Resources and Downloads." Bring out your Cootie Catchers (page 82) and Paper Dice (page 77) for a truly unique experience.

17. Whose Nose Is That?

Target Skills: Vocabulary, Family Identification, Possession, Self-Identity

Materials: A full-face photograph of each family member printed to 8 x 10 inches (20 x 25 cm). *Optional*: A computer screen or tablet screen large enough to expand an image to life-size.

Object of the Game: Using photographs, the child will identify herself and family members as well as facial features.

Step One: Take separate full-face photographs of each family member.
- At a minimum, take pictures of your face and your baby's face.
- Include family pets.

Step Two: Place your child comfortably on your lap or in a position where you can both easily see the pictures.
- Looking at a picture of your own face, point out the different facial features.
  - "Whose nose is that? That's Mommy's nose!"
  - Touch your nose. Make a funny noise. (*Beep!*)
  - Invite her to touch your nose. Make a funny noise. (*Beep!*)
- Looking at a picture of your child's face, point out the different facial features.
  - "Whose nose is that? That's baby's nose!"
  - Touch her nose. Make a funny noise. (*Beep!*)
  - Invite her to touch her nose. Make a funny noise. (*Beep!*)

Step Three: Repeat the sequence with each facial feature, making a different funny noise for each one. Kiss or tickle each part as you feel appropriate. This is a tactile as well as verbal experience for parent and child.
- Basic facial features:
  - Eyes
  - Nose
  - Mouth
  - Hair
  - Ears
  - Neck
- Don't be afraid to add some "advanced" facial features in your play when the child is ready:

- Nostrils (Kids love this word for some reason.)
- Cheeks
- Forehead
- Eyebrows
- Earlobes (Another crowd-pleaser.)

Step Four: Vary the game to include siblings, grandparents, and pets, if they are present. This will usually result in giggles all around.

18. Feelings Finder

Babies are born with feelings and emotions that they need to communicate. Along with the words to express these emotions, they must also learn that other people have emotions, too. This supports the child's growing sense of identity. Becoming adept at reading the emotions of others lays the foundation for adult skills, like interpreting social cues and empathizing. This is a game that can be played even with preverbal children. Receptive vocabulary develops much earlier than expressive vocabulary, so it is never too early to play this game.

Target Skills: Empathy Development, Reading Facial Expressions, Emotional Vocabulary

Materials: Your own face; a towel, cloth, or paper large enough to cover your face; DIY "Peekaboo Emotional Expression Board" or DIY "Emotional Expression Card Deck" (poster board or a sturdy cloth large enough to display twelve playing cards, construction paper or an opaque cloth, safe nontoxic glue or tape). I have included a set of emotion cards to get you started. *Optional*: A list of facial expressions for easy-to-read emotions.

Object of the Game: The child will learn to identify the facial expressions and body language of others, as well as use these expressions to communicate her own emotions.

Step One: Collect pictures or photographs of human faces showing the most easily read emotions. You may find these pictures in children's books, magazines, or family albums. If you are confident in your drawing skills, try your hand at drawing them. There are also emojis and sticker sets that are readily available. Try a few options and see what works best for you and your child.

Make the images the same size. A standard playing card measures 3.5 x 2.5 inches (9 x 6 cm), so an image that is 2 inches square (6 cm square) should be good for the two formats I describe below.

- Easily read emotions:
    - Sad
    - Happy
    - Grumpy/Annoyed
    - Sleepy
    - Angry
    - Worried
    - Scared
    - Surprised
    - Excited
    - Silly
    - Bored
    - Tired
    - Hurt
    - Proud
    - Nervous

Step Two: To Create a "Peekaboo Emotional Expression Board":

- Use nontoxic glues and soft-as-possible materials, as very young children love to explore with their taste buds.
- Paste or tape the emotion expression pictures in four rows of three on a piece of poster board or sturdy cloth, well spaced so that you and your child can access the pictures easily and without confusion.
    - For a variation, you can paste or tape the pictures onto a deck of playing cards, one per each card.

- Be sure that the reverse side of all playing cards is the same design.
- Label each picture with the emotion.
- Cut rectangular pieces of opaque cloth or construction paper large enough to completely cover the surface of a playing card, one for each emotional expression picture.
  - 2.75 x 3.75 inches (7 x 10 cm)
- Glue or tape the cloth at the top edge of the faces on the sheet of poster board.
  - If you are using pictures glued to playing cards, you can skip this step.
  - The paper or cloth makes a flap that can be lifted to reveal the picture and the label.
  - Be sure that the pictures and the written emotion labels are completely covered.

Step Three: Time to explore. Choose one of the pictures. Turn the card over or lift the flap to reveal the face. Encourage your child to do it. Choose a word or phrase to repeat when a face is revealed. "Surprise " or "Peekaboo!" or "Yay!"—anything that will communicate interest and a bit of excitement to engage your child. You want her to be excited to see the different faces.

Step Four: Imitate the facial expressions and label the expressions as you do. Encourage her to mimic you. Celebrate when she does it. "It's a happy face. I can make a happy face . . . Can you? Wow! That's a great happy face."

Step Five: Encourage your child to explore the faces herself by lifting the flaps and making the faces. Play a game in which she makes the face and you guess which emotion it is. Let her guess your emotions if she has the words.

Step Six: You may find that some children are born em-
pathizers who cry when others cry. If your child becomes
upset, be sure to immediately stop. Comfort her and show
her that this is just a game. Show her a positive emotion.
Let her have a turn to show you an emotion. She will
quickly learn to enjoy playacting with you.

19. Nothing More Than Feelings

Target Skills: Empathy Development, Reading Facial Expressions, Emotional Vocabulary

Materials: DIY "Emotional Expression Card Deck," or a
list of facial expressions for easy-to-read emotions

Object of the Game: This game can be played with as few
as two players or with a larger group. All players will use
facial expressions and body language to communicate their
own emotions and identify those of others.

Step One: Use Smooshing (page 103) or the Riffle Shuffle
(page 104) to randomize the emotion cards.

Step Two: Place the cards facedown in five rows of three.

Step Three: Player One selects a card from the "game
board." Without revealing her card, she must communicate
the pictured emotion using her facial expressions and body
language. No sounds.

Step Four: The other players call out the name of the emotion they think she is showing.

Step Five: If one of the players correctly names the emotion, Player One gets a point for her acting.

Step Six: Everyone joins together to act out the emotion. (This step usually involves a lot of giggling.)

Step Seven: Play moves clockwise around the circle, with each player selecting a card and acting out the emotion.

Step Eight: The first player to get seven points wins.

20. Tell Me How You Feel

Target Skills: Empathy Development, Emotional Vocabulary, Similes and Synonyms

Materials: DIY Emotional Expression Card Deck. *Optional*: A list of facial expressions for easy-to-read emotions.

Object of the Game: This game can be played with as few as two players or with a larger group. All players will use similes and synonyms to label and communicate emotions.

Step One: Use Smooshing (page 103) or the Riffle Shuffle (page 104) to randomize the fifteen cards in the DIY Emotional Expression Card Deck.

Step Two: Place the cards facedown in five rows of three.

Step Three: Player One selects a card from the "game board." Without revealing her card, she must verbally communicate the pictured emotion through a phrase or simile.
- Example: The emotion is "Happy."
  - Synonym: Glad or Joyful
  - Simile: Over the moon!

Step Four: The other players call out the name of the emotion they think she is describing.

Step Five: If one of the players correctly names the emotion, Player One gets a point.

Step Six: Everyone joins together to act out the emotion. (This step is just too much fun to leave out.)

Step Seven: If no one is able to identify the emotion, the card is returned to the deck and the deck is reshuffled.

Step Eight: Play moves clockwise around the circle, with each player selecting a card and describing the emotion.

Step Nine: The first player to get seven points wins.

21. Who or What Am I?

Target Skills: Asking and Answering Yes/No Questions, Deductive Reasoning

Materials: Common-object picture cards (characters, animals, objects), card-holder headbands. *Optional*: Cards with pictures of famous people/places/things from popular culture or history.

Object of the Game: This game can be played with as few as two players or with a larger group. All players will ask a maximum of five questions to determine the identity of the character or animal in their headband. All players must answer each with accurate information.

Step One: Shuffle the deck of cards well (see the Riffle Shuffle, page 104).

Step Two: The person who is Player One covers her eyes and cannot peek.

Step Three: The dealer (adult) picks a card at random from the deck and places it in the headband facing out, so that all but Player One can see the picture.

Step Four: Player One then works clockwise (to the left) around the table, asking each player one question about the object/animal/person on the card that can be answered only with a "yes" or "no"(e.g., "Do I have a crown?"; "Am I yellow?"; "Do I roar?").

Player One has five chances to guess who/what she is to gain a point. If she is correct, the card is placed faceup in front of her.

Step Five: Game play moves to the next player clockwise (left) around the table. Player Two is given a headband and the dealer repeats Step One.

Step Six: The first player to earn three points is the winner.

22. All About You

Target Skills: Making Factual Statements, Deductive Reasoning, Listening for Descriptive Details

Materials: Common-object picture cards (characters, animals, objects), card-holder headband. *Optional*: Cards with pictures of famous people/places/things from popular culture or history.

Object of the Game: The player will determine the object on the hidden card based on five hints provided by the other players.

Step One: Shuffle the deck of cards well (see the Riffle Shuffle, page 104).

Step Two: The person who is Player One covers her eyes and cannot peek.

Step Three: The dealer (adult) picks a card at random from the deck and places it in the headband facing out, so that all but Player One can see the picture.

Step Four: Player One then works clockwise (to the left) around the table. Each player in turn can tell Player One a single piece of descriptive information about her card.

For example, Player One has a card showing a red apple. The hints from Player Two might be "You eat it," or "It is red."

Step Five: Player One has five chances to guess who or what she is to gain a point. If she is correct, the card is placed faceup in front of her.

Step Six: Game play moves to the next player clockwise (left) around the table. Player Two is given a headband and the dealer repeats Step One.

Step Seven: The first player to earn three points is the winner.

Note: "Who am I?" and "Who are you?" are fun games to play at birthday parties and family gatherings with players of all ages. For gatherings of more than five people, each player can be given a card-holder headband and a mystery card. As they mingle among the partygoers, they ask each a binary (yes/no) question or get one piece of information about their card. The first person to guess who or what she is wins the game, and a candy. (It *is* a party, after all!)

23. Clay Makers

Kids of all ages love working with clay. There are many commercial products on the market, but why not make your own? For very young "mouth explorers," homemade edible play dough is a great alternative. For older children, making their own dough is a chance to explore color combinations as they gain pride in their accomplishment.

There are recipes for homemade play dough available on the internet that you may choose to consider. I have included two recipes that are easy-to-make classics. Both recipes are edible. However, please be aware of any possible allergies when selecting the recipe you want to use. When in doubt, consult your pediatrician.

Target Skills: Following Directions, Vocabulary for Math (Measurement, Addition, Subtraction), Color (Mixing)

Materials: Food coloring (red, green, yellow, blue), a bowl for each color play dough, measuring spoons and cups, plastic wrap or sandwich bags, plastic or latex gloves (for handling food coloring), the ingredients based on the selected recipe

Recipe One: Basic Play Dough: Cold water, salt, vegetable oil, food coloring, flour, cornstarch

Recipe Two: Long-Lasting Play Dough: Water, vegetable oil, salt, cream of tartar, food coloring, flour

Object of the Game: This is a make-it-and-use-it activity that teaches your child resourcefulness through math and art. In the end she will have something she can use.

Step One: Have your child assist you in gathering the ingredients and materials based on the recipe you will be using. Set out a small bowl for each ingredient in preparation for measuring. Place everything within easy reach on the counter or table. Plan to have one mixing bowl for each color play dough you plan to make, and expand the recipe accordingly.

Step Two: This is the "art-science" portion of this activity. Take some time to explore color combinations and plan how many different colors you will make. (Now is a good time to wear the gloves.) Experiment with color-combining using the three primary colors red, blue, and yellow. From these three primary colors you can create three secondary colors.

- Red + Blue = Purple
- Red + Yellow = Orange
- Blue + Yellow = Green

Demonstrate color-mixing by dropping one drop of red and one drop of blue in a cup of water.

- Ask your child to predict what color you will make from each combination.
- Will the colors be different if you add more of one primary color than the other?
- What happens if you mix all the primary colors?

Step Three: Assist your child in measuring out the ingredients for the recipe you have chosen and the number of colors you are going to prepare. For our example, we will use Recipe One: Basic Play Dough.

Step Four: Combine the ingredients as directed in the recipe.

Recipe One: Basic Play Dough (One Color)

INGREDIENTS

1 cup cold water
1 cup salt
2 teaspoons vegetable oil
  Red, yellow, and blue food coloring
3 cups flour
2 tablespoons cornstarch

DIRECTIONS

Optional: Put on the plastic/latex gloves.

1. Mix together the water, salt, oil, and enough food coloring to make a bright color in a large bowl.
2. Gradually add the flour and cornstarch.
3. Knead the mixture with your hands until it feels and looks like bread dough.
4. Store covered with plastic wrap or in a sandwich bag.

Step Five: The number of colors you choose to make is up to you. I recommend that you plan to make at least the three primary colors red, yellow, and blue. Your child can mix colors after the play dough is prepared by squishing two play dough color balls together until they combine well. The choice is yours.

Step Six: Here is a recipe for play dough that can last up to six months because it includes cream of tartar. If you don't include this ingredient you will not get the result you are seeking. You will also need a saucepan. This one requires a bit of cooking.

Recipe Two: Long-Lasting Play Dough (One Color)

INGREDIENTS

1 cup water
1 tablespoon vegetable oil
½ cup salt
1 tablespoon cream of tartar
Food coloring
1 cup flour

DIRECTIONS

1. In a medium saucepan, combine the water, oil, salt, cream of tartar, and food coloring.
2. Heat over a low to medium burner until the mixture is warm.
3. Remove the pan from the stove.
4. Add the flour.
5. Stir well until the mixture is not hot to the touch.
6. Knead the dough until smooth (the texture of bread dough).
7. Store this dough covered in plastic wrap or in a sandwich bag. Should last up to six months.

24. Michelangelo

Target Skills: Following Directions, Problem Solving, Comparison, Critical Thinking, Verbal Reasoning

Materials: Enough homemade play dough or clay for each player to have (at least) the three primary colors to create a sculpture, a smooth nonstick working surface, large books to serve as barriers for each player, one paper bag, a timer

Optional: Rolling pins; plastic knives, spoons, and forks; a variety of cookie cutters.

Object of the Game: Each player must produce a sculpture based on a photograph or illustration that is recognizable to the other players. If the player is successful, she has earned the right to be called a Michelangelo.

Step One: Cut out a variety of pictures from your gathered sources (magazines, old storybook illustrations, family photos).

- The number selected is equal to the number of players plus one.
- Fold the pictures into roughly the same size squares.
- Place them in the bag.
- Player One closes the bag by crumpling the top and shakes the bag well to randomize the contents.

Step Two: Set up your working surfaces and barriers. Each player must have enough room to work without another player being able to see what she is doing. A dining room table is usually good for up to four players.

Step Three: Starting with Player Two, each player selects a picture from the bag but does not share it with the others. This is the picture each is tasked with creating as a play dough sculpture.

Step Four: Set the timer for a period of time long enough for your players to create their sculptures.

- Between ten and fifteen minutes should be enough.
- As you start the timer, say, "Go!"
- This is the cue to begin their creations.

Step Five: As the timer counts down, the players create their sculptures behind the barriers.

When the timer stops, everyone must stop sculpting.

Step Six: All players refold their source pictures and place them back in the paper bag.
- Player One shakes the bag to randomize the pictures.
- Starting with Player Two, each player selects a picture from the bag, but doesn't show it to anyone.
- If a player gets the picture of her own sculpture, she folds it up again and places it back in the bag, then selects another picture.

Step Seven: Once everyone has a picture, take down the barriers and reveal the sculptures.
- Move materials out of the way so that everyone has a clear view of each other's sculpture.
- Take a moment to admire each other's work.

Step Eight: At this point all players reveal the picture they must match to the other players' sculptures.
- Starting with Player One, each player selects a sculpture that they think matches their picture.
- She must say why she thinks it is the right sculpture.
  - E.g., "My picture has a man with a red hat, and Ellie's sculpture has a red hat."

Step Nine: Identifying Michelangelo
- If Player One is correct, it is Ellie, the creator of the sculpture, who is congratulated and awarded the title of Michelangelo.
  - Remember to cheer for Ellie's achievement.
  - "Yay! Good job, Ellie!"
- Player One gets a point for being a keen observer who can explain why the sculpture goes with her picture.

- If Player One is incorrect, game play moves to Player Two, who now must identify the sculpture that goes with her picture.
- Play continues until each player has identified the creator of the sculpture that goes with their picture.

25. Paper Dice

Target Skills: Following Directions, Problem Solving, Creative Thinking, Math Vocabulary

Materials: Scissors; rectangular writing paper, construction paper, or card stock; tape or glue; a marker, pen, or pencil. *Optional*: Emoji or character stickers.

Sometimes it is useful to customize a set of dice, or to design a single die that will suit your needs and make game play move forward without fuss. This blank die pattern can be used in as many creative ways as you and your child can dream up. Just as with the Cootie Catcher (page 82), it is up to you. Have fun making them and using them. I have included some suggestions to get you started.

You can use the following template to easily make and customize a dice set from a standard sheet of writing paper, construction paper, or card stock. (This template can also be downloaded at simonandschuster.com/books/The-Gift -of-Gab.)

Step One: Copy the template by tracing or using a photocopier. Although standard writing paper will work fine, it is recommended that you use construction paper or card stock to build a sturdier set of dice. Print out two copies of the blank die template.

Step Two: Cut out the cube templates along the outer edge. Small children will find this a fun challenge to strengthen

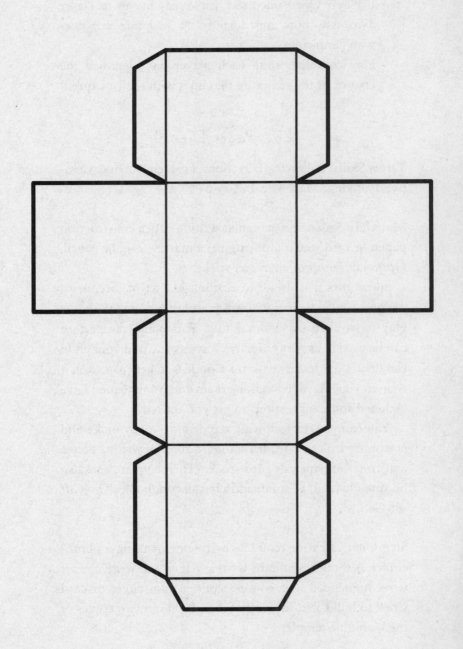

their fine motor skills. You can always clean up their edges before Step Three.

Step Three: Fold the small flaps for each face of the cube template along the inside lines to the wrong side of the cube face. Test the folds to be sure that when completed they will form a cube with six sides.

Step Four: Each of the die's six faces now present an opportunity to customize your die for the game you wish to play. There are limitless options. Here are a few suggestions:
- Mimic a standard set of game dice by drawing a different number of dots (one to six) on each face.
  - You can draw dots or make other fun shapes like flowers, stars, hearts, or smiley faces.
  - Create a standard set of numbered dice using Arabic numerals (1, 2, 3, 4, 5, 6) on each face.
  - Be sure the numbers on the opposite faces of the die add up to seven.
  - A pair of numbered dice can be used to practice basic addition and subtraction.
- Create one standard die and reserve one die for words, phrases, or pictures. The numbered die can be used in many ways. For example, it can be used to assign points for a correct response to a game question, or to determine how many times a player must say a phrase.
- Or you can use one die, as described in the samples below, to create a game of your own design.
  - Write a Part of Speech word on each face of the die.
    - Noun, Verb, Adjective, Article, Adverb, Prefix, Suffix
  - Write a Word Phrase on each face of the die.
    - Noun + Verb, Adjective + Noun, Verb + Object Noun, Noun + Past-tense Verb

- Prepositional Phrase (in, on, from, to, at, under, over)
- Write a category name on each face of the die.
  - Animals, Plants, People (Occupations), Places, Tools, Clothing, etc.
  - Customize the categories to compliment a player's interests or the skill areas you want to strengthen.
- Write a chapter heading from a school text on each face of the die.
  - Roll the numbered die to ask the player to tell you up to six facts about that topic.
  - Customize the numbered die if six facts appear too challenging or unrealistic.
- Write a vocabulary or spelling word from the classroom on each face of the die.
  - The player must use the word in a sentence.
  - The player may look at the word for three seconds, then close her eyes and spell the word aloud.
- Use stickers or draw pictures on each face of the die to represent characters in a storytelling game.
  - King, Queen, Knight, Dragon, Farmer, Boy, Girl, etc.
  - Write a story starter phrase on each face of one die and a story extender/ending phrase on each face of the other.
    - Once Upon a Time, Deep in the Woods, Long Ago and Far Away, Just Last Week, Someday, Not Long from Now, I Wouldn't Have Believed It if I Hadn't Seen . . .
    - Meanwhile, And Then, But, In Conclusion, They Lived Happily Ever After
- Write a tongue twister on each face of the die.
- Write a Wh-Question form on each of the six faces.
  - Who, What, Where, When, Why, How

Step Five: Apply glue on the right side of one of the tabs, then fold and stick the tab to the wrong side of the adjacent die face. You may find that tape is more efficient for this step. You can choose double-sided sticky tape. If you choose one-sided sticky tape, make sure it is clear.

Step Six: Glue the rest of the faces together along the tabs to complete the die.

26. Question Time

Target Skills: Asking and Answering Wh-Questions, Grammar, Vocabulary, Reasoning

Materials: List of Who, What, Where, When, Why, and How questions, Paper Dice (page 77)

Object of the Game: When given a statement, the player will convert the sentence into a requested Wh-Question form. The first player to gain five points is the winner.

Step One: Prepare your Wh-Question Paper Dice as per Step Four on page 79.

Wh-Questions

- Who
- What
- Where
- When
- Why
- How

Step Two: Use Smooshing (page 103) or the Riffle Shuffle (page 104) to randomize the statement cards. Place the deck of statement cards facedown in the center of the table.

Step Three: Player One rolls the paper die and identifies the type of Wh-Question form she will need to create. For our example, the die face reads "Who."

Step Four: Player One takes the top card from the statement deck. For our example it reads:

- *After school, Bobby packed his bag and ran away from home because he wanted to join the circus.*

Step Five: Player One must now turn the statement into a "Who" question to gain the point. For our example:

- *Who ran away from home?*

Step Six: If Player One cannot provide the appropriate Wh-Question, the statement card remains faceup on the table and play moves clockwise to Player Two.

Step Seven: Player Two now rolls the Wh-die, identifies a question form, and selects the top card from the statement deck, repeating Steps Three through Five.

Step Eight: If Player Two is successful, she gets her point and has the opportunity to pick up an extra point by rolling the Wh-die and converting Player One's statement into the requested Wh-Question form.

Step Nine: Play proceeds clockwise around the table until a player gains five points and is declared the winner.

27. Cootie Catchers

When I was a kid these were called Fortune Tellers. In the preenlightened past, my friends and I loved to try to predict the future by using these to answer questions of utmost importance, like, "Who likes me?" or "Will I go to the prom?" When I began to use these with my students, I found that, while both boys and girls loved to use the "Fortune Tellers" in game play, only the girls would take this game and play it with their friends on the playground. The boys were less likely to share this game with friends, until, that is, the name of the game changed to "Cootie Catchers." Everyone, it seems, likes to catch cooties.

Target Skills: Following Directions, Problem Solving, Creative Thinking

Materials: Scissors, rectangular writing paper (construction or craft paper is often too thick), a marker, pen, or pencil. *Optional*: Emoji or character stickers.

Object of the Game: This is a multifaceted game that can be used in many ways for many purposes. The Cootie Catcher is a versatile tool. It can be used to determine who will be Player One ("Who goes first?"). By becoming creative with what is written or pictured on the folds, Cootie Catchers can also be used as an integral part of a game format to determine the question to be asked or answered or how many times a tongue twister must be said to win a point. I have included Cootie Catchers whenever possible as options in game play. Kids love them.

How to Build a Cootie Catcher

Although kindergarten-age children love using the Cootie Catcher, the creation of the Cootie Catcher can be a bit challenging, even for adults. If you are out of Cootie Catching practice, I strongly suggest that you practice making the Cootie Catcher a few times before teaching the kids how to do it. Cootie Catcher creation is a language lesson in following multistep directions.

You can visit simonandschuster.com/books/The-Gift-of -Gab to download a template for the Cootie Catcher, and follow the instructions below using a standard sheet of writing paper.

Step One: To square off the rectangular paper, fold the bottom left corner of the paper to the right side of the page to make a triangle, leaving a margin at the top of the fold.

Step Two: Cut off the margin at the top. When you unfold the paper, it should be square.

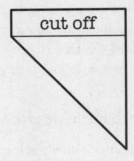

Step Three: Fold the lower left corner to the upper right corner. Then open. You should have a diagonal crease in the paper from the upper left to the lower right.

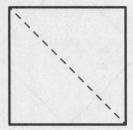

Step Four: Fold the lower right corner to the upper left corner. Then open. You now have a center point marked by the intersection of the two creases.

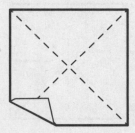

Step Five: Fold each corner of the square to the center point. You should now have a diamond-shaped square with the folds forming a cross.

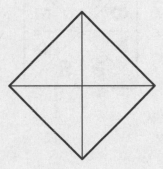

Step Six: Flip the paper over so that the folds are facedown on the table.

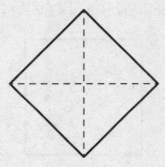

Step Seven: Fold each corner of the diamond to the center. When you are done you should have a square composed of eight triangles.

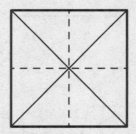

Step Eight: Write the numbers *1* through *8* on each of the triangles.

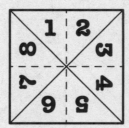

Step Nine: Fold the left side of the square to the right side, forming a vertical rectangle. Then unfold.

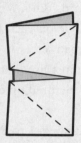

Step Ten: Fold the bottom of the square to the top to form a horizontal rectangle. Then unfold.

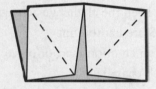

Step Eleven: Open each flap. Write something on each triangle. This is the side that tells the player the task she is to perform. The options are endless and can be designed to complement any language skill you want to feature. This is the challenge task, the one the player must complete to get the point(s).

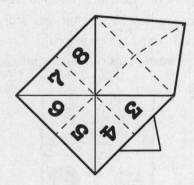

For example:
- Wh-Questions
  - Write the words Who, What, Where, When, Why, and How—one on each triangle. You can write them more than once.
  - The player must use that Wh-Question form to ask about a pictured object.
- Tongue Twister
  - Write the numbers *1* to *8* on each flap.
    - The number selected is the number of times the player must say each tongue twister for the point.
    - Write a tongue twister on each flap. Be sure to keep the challenge achievable.
- Emotional State Pantomime
  - Draw an emotion face, or place an emoji sticker on each triangle flap.
    - Happy, Sad, Confused, Curious, Afraid, Surprised, Disgusted, Angry
  - The player must pantomime the emotion selected so that the other players can guess what she is trying to communicate.

Step Twelve: Turn the Cootie Catcher over. You should have four flaps. Write something on each flap that complements the language skill you want to feature. This is the side of the Cootie Catcher that helps the player identify the task she is to perform. This can be anything you choose.

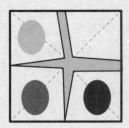

- First Name, Middle Name, Last Name, Parent's/Teacher's Name
  - The player manipulates the Cootie Catcher as she spells the name.
- Color: Red, Green, Blue, Yellow
  - The player must name something in the room that is the requested color.
  - She then manipulates the Cootie Catcher as she spells the name of the object.
- Name of a Place: City, Jungle, Desert, Forest
  - The player must name an animal or plant that lives in that environment.
  - She then manipulates the Cootie Catcher as she spells the name of the animal.

Step Thirteen: Turn the Cootie Catcher over. The triangles with the numbers from Step Eight should be faceup. Fold the square in half and place your thumbs and index fingers under the four flaps. You have now completed your Cootie Catcher!

28. Basic Cootie Catcher Game: How to Play

Target Skills: Asking and Answering Questions, Figurative Language, Problem Solving, Creative Thinking

Materials: Cootie Catcher, Getting to Know You Questions

Object of the Game: This game can be played with as few as two players or with a larger group.

The types of challenge tasks can vary according to each child's needs and interests. Establish the object of the game in Step One. Cootie Catchers can be used as fortune-tellers, to establish the order of play, or to make silly sentences. The method for their use is the same, but you are free to get as creative as you and your child wish.

Step One: Establish what the first question will be based on the design of your Cootie Catcher as per Step Twelve of "How to Build a Cootie Catcher" (page 88). There are many options for questions to ask if an individual player has more than one turn with the Cootie Catcher. For example:

- First Name, Middle Name, Last Name, Parent's/ Teacher's Name
- Color: Red, Green, Blue, Yellow
- Name/Picture of a Place: City, Jungle, Desert, Forest

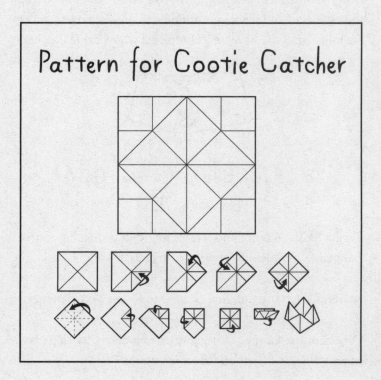

Pattern for Cootie Catcher

Step Two: Player One slips her fingers into the flaps as directed in Step Thirteen of "How to Build a Cootie Catcher" (page 89).

Step Three: Player One provides an answer to the question. Then, moving the flaps in and out and side to side in time with the letters, she spells out the word she has chosen.

Step Four: Open the Cootie Catcher to reveal the numbers. Player One selects a number.

Step Five: Player One counts out the number she has chosen while moving the flaps in and out and side to side.

Step Six: Repeat Step Five to randomize the process even further.

Step Seven: Player One picks a number. This is the number of points she wins if she meets the challenge.

Step Eight: Player One opens the flap to reveal the challenge task you have written on the inside flap.

Step Nine: Once Player One completes the challenge task, the Cootie Catcher is passed to Player Two who repeats Steps One through Eight.

29. Ask the Right Question and Get the Right Answer

In school, a child is often called on to answer a question based on a textbook chapter or written paragraph. This poses a challenge for some children who have difficulty establishing just what the teacher wants them to say. This can lead to a written or verbal "word salad," where the child talks and talks, hoping to hit it lucky and get the right answer. The basic technique this game is designed to teach, taking a question form and inverting it to create a declarative sentence, is a gateway to auditory and reading comprehension. Once a child has mastered this technique, she will use it from first grade through high school.

This technique makes it much easier to find requested information in what is often a long and boring text. It also fosters the use of correct grammar in written composition. I encouraged my own children (okay, I forced them) to write out the questions first, as well as the answers, when I supervised their homework. They hated it. I won't lie to you. They did, however, come to appreciate having writing skills that they continue to use in their adult professions.

Target Skills: Categorization, Associations, Wh-Question Formulation, Declarative Sentence Structure

Materials: Object Noun Cards, a Cootie Catcher, playing dice

Object of the Game: To formulate a Wh-Question and complete a declarative sentence that gives the requested information.

- Example 1
    - Question: Who wrote *Alice in Wonderland*?
    - Response: *Alice in Wonderland* was written by Lewis Carroll. (Advanced response: Charles Lutwidge Dodgson.)
- Example 2
    - Name an example of an animal that has striped fur.
    - An example of an animal that has striped fur is a skunk.

Step One: Create a Cootie Catcher using the pattern provided with this book. On the inside surfaces write the words Who, What, Where, When, Why, and How, one word on each panel of the Cootie Catcher.

Step Two: Select cards appropriate to your child's interest and knowledge level from the Object Noun Deck. You will need at least twenty cards to start play. This game uses the Object Noun Deck of pictures (people/places/things) as a starting point. I encourage you to expand this deck or create your own to suit your child's interests.

Step Three: Shuffle the cards well three to five times and place the deck in the center of the table.

Step Four: Player One takes the top card from the deck and places it faceup on the table for all players to see.

Step Five: Player One rolls the die. The revealed number dictates the number of times she must alternate the Cootie Catcher to reveal the type of Wh-Question (Who/What/Where/When/Why/How) she must formulate. (See "Basic Cootie Catcher Game," page 89, or "Paper Dice," page 77.)

Step Six: Player Two must answer the Wh-Question using an appropriate and complete declarative sentence.
   Example questions and appropriate responses:
   • Selected card shows a motorcycle.
      • Who rides a motorcycle?
         • My dad rides a motorcycle.
      • What do you need to ride a motorcycle?
         • You need a helmet and a leather jacket to ride a motorcycle.

- Why would a police officer ride a motorcycle?
  - A police officer would ride a motorcycle to catch a bad guy.
- Where do people ride motorcycles?
  - People ride motorcycles on the highway.
- When do people ride motorcycles?
  - People ride motorcycles to go to work in the morning.

Step Seven: Player One gets one point for formulating a correct Wh-Question. Player Two gets one point for formulating a correct declarative sentence in response.

Step Eight: Play moves to Player Two, who takes the next card from the deck, rolls the die, and uses the Cootie Catcher to select a Wh-Question type to ask Player Three about the pictured object.

Step Nine: The first player to get twelve points is the winner.

30. Cupid's Coming

Target Skills: Alphabetizing, Parts of Speech, Prefixes and Suffixes, Verb Tenses, Question Formulation

Materials: Twenty-six cards, each with a letter of the alphabet written on it; a pair of dice; Wh-Question Cootie Catcher. *Optional*: Paper and pencil or color chips (red for correct question, blue for correct answer) to track points.

Object of the Game: The first player to get six asking points and six answering points wins.

Step One: Prepare your Wh-Question Cootie Catcher as per Step Eleven Wh-Questions of "How to Build a Cootie Catcher" (page 87).

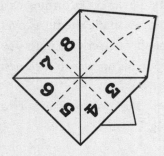

Write the words Who, What, Why, Where, When, and How—one on each triangle. You can write them more than once to fill out the Cootie Catcher.

Step Two: Shuffle the alphabet cards well three to five times (see Riffle Shuffle, page 104, or Smooshing, page 103) and place the deck facedown in the center of the table.

Step Three: To start, Player One plays the "Basic Cootie Catcher Game" (page 89) to identify the type of Wh-Question that Player Two must ask.

- Ask Player One to pick one of the four colors shown on the flaps.
- Moving the flaps in and out and side to side in time with the letters, Player One spells out the chosen color.
- Player One opens the Cootie Catcher to reveal the numbers, and picks one. He then counts out the number as he moves the flaps in and out and side to side.
- This time, Player One picks a second number, opens the flap, and reveals the type of Wh-Question that Player Two must ask.
    - For our example, he has landed on "When."

Step Four: Player Two rolls the dice to get a number between *2* and *12*. For our example she rolls an *11*. She counts out the number as she removes the cards one by one from the top of the deck, turning card eleven over for all to see. For our example she turns over a *Y*. That is the letter of the alphabet Player One must use to start the most important word in his answer to the question "When."

Step Five: Player One turns to Player Two and announces, "Cupid's coming."

Step Six: Player Two responds, "When will he come?"

Step Seven: Player One responds, "Cupid <u>came</u> yesterday." Note that the player must adjust the verb tense to agree with the word "yesterday" in his answer. Players get one point for each correct question or answer.

Step Eight: Shuffle the card deck.

Step Nine: Player Two now uses the Cootie Catcher to identify the Wh-Question that Player Three must ask. Player Three rolls the dice to select the letter of the alphabet Player Two must use in her answer.

Step Ten: Play proceeds clockwise around the table until the first player has earned six question points and six answer points.

7. WHO GOES FIRST?

TAKING TURNS AND COOPERATION

By the time children reach kindergarten age, they enjoy group games that are rule-governed. For some reason, establishing who goes first is of greatest importance as a marker of fair play. School-age children have a fairness radar that must be reckoned with, therefore before you begin playing any game, establish a means of determining who goes first. Adults may automatically give in to a child's demand to go first, but other children? Not so much. Establishing who goes first can become a nightmare. As a young, inexperienced speech pathologist, I found myself in the middle of arguments with students about fairness that would take up valuable time, accomplishing nothing but hurt feelings and frustration.

Then I remembered how my dad handled these things. Good ol' Dad! He taught me time-honored ways of establishing a starting point that every child can master. In fact, children have been using them for centuries. I applied my own flourish to use these pre-game games as language-building exercises. The best part is that the kids never realized that there was some adult goal setting going on.

NO MATERIALS NECESSARY:
MORE METHODS TO ENSURE FAIRNESS

Sometimes a set of dice or a deck of cards is not readily available. Never fear! There are time-tested favorites that require nothing more than hands. I have introduced two generations of kids to these methods. These games will never disappear from the playground.

31. One Potato-Two Potato

Target Skills: Asking and Answering Questions, Spelling, Turn-taking, Personal Identification Details

Materials: Hands

Object of the Game: Players will use their spelling and general knowledge skills to determine who goes first.

Step One: Before starting play, establish a question (or questions) of the day. This could be anything appropriate, such as: "What is your middle name?"; "What is your favorite book?"; "What celebrity would you like to meet someday?"; "What street do you live on?"; "What is your father/mother/brother/sister's name?"; "What is your best talent?"

Step Two: Instruct the children to "stick out your potatoes." Demonstrate by making fists with both of your hands, placing them in the center of the table in front of you.

Step Three: Touch your right hand to your chin, then to your left hand, working your way around the circle, touching each child's hand in succession as you say each number in the chant.

> *"One potato, two potato, three potato, four,*
> *five potato, six potato, seven potato, more."*

Step Four: Stop at the child whose hand is touched as you chant, "More."

Step Five: Now is the fun part. Ask that child the day's question. ("What is your middle name?" "William.")

Step Six: Spell the name W-I-L-L-I-A-M as you continue to touch each child's "potatoes" with each letter. The potato you land on is then called "out" and placed behind that child's back.

Step Seven: Begin the "potato" chant again, as in Step Three, starting with the next "potato" in the circle.

Step Eight: If the chant of "More" lands on the same child, no problem. Ask your second question of the day.

Step Nine: The game continues until only one potato remains. That child now goes first and the game you have selected proceeds clockwise around the table (to the left).

Step Ten: As the children become more familiar with the process and more sophisticated in answering questions, they can ask the day's question(s) of the group member of their choice when their "potato" is selected at "More," or they can spell their answer to the day's question(s) as you tap the "potatoes."

32. Inka-Dinka Bottle of Inka

Target Skills: Asking and Answering Questions, Spelling, Turn-taking, Personal Identification

Materials: Hands, question cards

Sample Question Ideas

- What is your middle name?
- What is your favorite book?
- What celebrity would you like to meet someday?
- What is your best talent?
- What is your superpower?
- What street do you live on?
- How many brothers and/or sisters do you have?

Object of the Game: Players will use their spelling and general knowledge skills to determine who goes first.

Step One: Before starting play, place the question cards in the center of the table.

Step Two: The children are instructed to "stick out your stinkers." They make fists with both hands and place them on the table.

Step Three: Touch your right hand to your chin, then to your left hand, working your way around the circle, touching each child's hand in succession as you say each word in the chant.

> *"Inka-dinka bottle of inka,*
> *cap fell off and you stinka."*

Step Four: Touch each child's hand in succession, working around the table with each beat of the chant. Stop at the child whose hand is touched as you chant, "Stinka."

Step Five: Now is the fun part. The "stinka" picks a question card from the pile and asks the child to his left (clockwise) to answer the question (e.g., "What is your middle name?" . . . "William"). This method ensures that each child has an opportunity to ask a question, as well as answer a question.

Step Six: Spell the name W-I-L-L-I-A-M as you continue to touch each child's "stinkas." The "stinka" you land on with the last letter is then called "out" and placed behind that child's back.

Step Seven: Begin the "inka-dinka" chant again, as in Step Three, starting with the next "stinka" in the circle. This process continues until only one "stinka" remains. That child now goes first in the day's game with play proceeding clockwise around the table.

33. It's a Crap Shoot: Tossing Dice

It sounds so simple. All you need is a set of dice, right? Not so fast. There are some concepts your child must learn before throwing those dice.

Target Skills: Math Concepts (Odd/Even, Less Than/Greater Than, Highest/Lowest, More/Fewer, Pattern Recognition, One to One Correspondence, Number Values), Fairness

Materials: Playing dice. *Optional*: Paper Dice (page 77).

Object of the Game: Players will use their knowledge of relative value to determine who goes first.

Step One: Ensure that everyone knows how to count the dots. For very young players (age four or five), you may need to use a large set of dice so they can use their fingers to keep track of the dots as they count.

Step Two: Firmly establish the concepts of greater than and less than. This is usually a bit easier. Kids as young as age three or four understand that six is older (more) than five, and five is older than four. You can build on that.

Step Three: You will need to provide some basic instruction on the proper way to roll the dice. There's a troublemaker in every group who enjoys sending the dice off the table. It's fun to watch everyone scramble to find the dice. Do some bud-nipping by establishing a rule that you will subtract one point for each die that rolls off the table. That usually works after the first try.

Option: Place the dice in a clear plastic container that provides enough room for the dice to jiggle and randomize. The "thrower" can then fiercely jiggle the dice and place the container firmly on the table to read the numbers without the option of throwing them off the table. This is a good option for small hands and large dice.

Step Four: The player who rolls the highest number goes first, then play moves clockwise (to the left) around the table.

Step Five: In case of a tie, those two players toss the dice again. Repeat the process until a "winner" is chosen.

A deck of playing cards is a beautiful thing. From the Middle Ages to the present, people all over the world enjoy the look, feel, and sound of playing cards. Las Vegas depends on it. Their slot machines try to duplicate the satisfying sound of shuffling cards. Kids are fascinated with the dexterity required in executing the Riffle Shuffle (page 104) and will spend hours practicing. Then there is the exploration of randomness that results from a good shuffle. When you combine that random quality with a rule-based game, you have golden opportunities for language expansion.

34. Smooshing

A method of randomizing cards that is fun for smaller children is called Smooshing. The rules are simple, and the action is fierce, a combination that kids can't resist.

Target Skills: Following Directions, Cooperation, Reciting a Rhyme or Singing a Short Song

Materials: A standard deck of fifty-two cards or a deck of game-specific playing cards. *Optional*: An egg timer or the timer on a cell phone.

Object of the Game: Players will work together to randomize a card deck.

Step One: Allocate all the cards from the deck among the players. It doesn't have to be exactly divided, just fairly distributed.

Step Two: Each player pushes his cards to the center of the table and begins to smoosh the cards around, moving them in a single layer to the player to his left as he smooshes cards taken from the player to his right.

Step Three: Continue smooshing the cards around the tabletop for a specified period of time. This can be the time it takes to sing "Happy Birthday," "Mary Had a Little Lamb," "Twinkle Twinkle Little Star," or any favorite song. If you are not musical, you can recite a short poem or tell a knock-knock joke. If all else fails, you can use a timer to set a time limit of thirty to sixty seconds. That ought to allow enough time to randomize the deck.

Step Four: When the song is done or the timer goes off, all players push the cards into the center of the table.

Step Five: The dealer stacks the cards neatly and deals them out to the players according to the rules of the game to be played.

35. The Riffle Shuffle

I admit it. The Riffle Shuffle is my favorite trick to teach kids. It is a challenging fine motor skill that kids can use to impress and amaze their friends. It is a challenge worth mastering. Riffle Shuffling five to seven times is the best and quickest way to truly randomize a deck of cards.

Target Skills: Following Complex Directions, Card Vocabulary, Physical Vocabulary (finger digits), Advanced Vocabulary (Rifling, Curve, Concave, and Convex), Number and Assigned Values

Materials: A standard deck of fifty-two playing cards or a deck of game-specific playing cards

Object of the Game: Players will follow a series of challenging directions to randomize a card deck.

Before instructing the child, demonstrate the steps for the Riffle Shuffle.

Step One: Divide the deck into two equal stacks.

Step Two: Take half the deck in each hand with the thumb over the top edge and your middle and ring finger at the bottom edge.

Step Three: Bend your index finger over the deck for support.

Step Four: Gently bend each half of the deck so it becomes curved with the middle bending inward.

Step Five: Riffle the deck with your thumbs by bending the half decks a bit more and using your thumbs to move slowly upward along the edge of the cards. The cards in the two decks will riffle together, creating a shuffled deck.

Step Six: Repeat Steps One through Five several times, describing each step slowly and deliberately.

Step Seven: By this time your child will be begging you to let him try. Hand the deck of cards to him. Supervise him as he goes through Steps One through Five.

Step Eight: Once he is satisfied that he knows all the steps, leave him to practice independently. He will be happy to show everyone what he can do once he masters the Riffle Shuffle.

Step Nine: The dealer stacks the cards neatly and deals them out to the players according to the rules of the game to be played.

36. Pick a Card, Any Card

Target Skills: Math Concepts (Odd/Even, Less than/Greater than, Highest/Lowest), Card Terms, Symbolic Meaning

Materials: A standard deck of fifty-two playing cards

Object of the Game: Players will use their knowledge of relative value to determine who goes first.

Step One: Kids love stories about kings, queens, and knights. Playing cards feature those fabled characters. Although many young children may have seen adults playing games with standard playing cards, they may not be familiar with how these cards are designed. This is an opportunity for terrific conversations. Start by exploring the four suits: hearts (red), spades (black), clubs (black), and diamonds (red).

Step Two: Discuss how each suit has thirteen cards: one to ten, a king, a queen, and a jack. Most decks also have two joker cards included. Instruction in relative value of playing cards must be established. Spend some time sorting the cards into the suits, ordering them from ace to king. Which is of more value, an ace or a king? A jack or a ten? When would you use the joker? Introduce the concept of a wild card.

You may find yourself discussing why the cards are named for royal offices. Let the kids guide the conversation with their questions. (You may have to google some of the answers.)

Step Three: Before playing any game with the cards, all players must agree on their relative values. I think the most obvious way is the best.

- King: 13 points
- Queen: 12 points
- Knave/Jack: 11 points
- Number cards at face value: Ace = 1 point, to 10 = 10 points.
- When playing a game, the ace can be the wild card, with a value of 1 or 14, as the player wishes according to the agreed-upon rules for that game.

Step Four: Review the role of the adult as dealer and how this establishes fairness. Once you have established the relative card values, the dealer shuffles (see the Riffle Shuffle, page 104, or Smooshing, page 103) the cards one time for each player, asking the player to approve the shuffle by tapping the deck before moving on to the next player/shuffle. This firmly establishes the fairness of the shuffle. Randomization is accomplished with three to seven shuffles.

Step Five: Place the deck in the center of the table. The dealer then deals a card to each player. The player with the highest-value card goes first, with play proceeding clockwise around the table (to the left).

Step Six: In case of a tie, those two players are dealt an additional card. The value of each player's two cards are totaled, with the highest value going first. Repeat the process until a winner is chosen.

8. A FULL DECK

CARD GAMES FOR EVERY OCCASION

Cards, especially customized cards, are flexible game materials that can be used for almost any time, place, interest, or skill level.

37. Classic Memory

Target Skills: Short-term Memory, Following Simple Directions, Vocabulary

Materials: Common-object and/or action-verb picture cards, two cards for each pictured item or action. For best play, select six to ten pairs of cards.

Object of the Game: Find matching pairs of pictured objects and/or actions from a grid or a scatter of "hidden" cards.

Step One: Select the recommended number of paired playing cards from your preferred decks.

Step Two: Shuffle all cards together at least three times to randomize the deck.

Step Three: Place the cards facedown on the table. For younger children, or if memory skills are your primary concern, I recommend that you place the cards in an orderly grid pattern to facilitate short-term memory. For more advanced or older children, you can choose to scatter the cards facedown on the table.

Step Four: Player One selects two cards from the grid and turns them faceup.

- He must name the object or action pictured on the cards.
- If he has found two different objects or actions, he places the cards facedown where he found them.
- If he has found a matched pair, he takes the cards, places them in front of him, and gets the point.
  - Remember to celebrate with a little cheer to reward his effort.

Step Five: Play continues clockwise (to the left) until all matched pairs are found. The player who finds the most matched pairs is the winner.

38. Family Finder

Target Skills: Short-term Memory, Following Simple Directions, Visual Discrimination, Vocabulary, Family Relationships

Materials: Common-object and/or action-verb picture cards or a standard deck of fifty-two playing cards (at least four times as many cards as there are family members; e.g., for a family of four you would want at least sixteen cards); photographs of individual family members, small enough to fit each one on a playing card

Object of the Game: Find all of the family members' photographs from a grid or a scatter of "hidden" cards.

Step One: Select the recommended number of playing cards from your preferred decks. Take one card per family member and tape, or glue, if you prefer a permanent playing card, a family member's photograph to the playing side of the card.

Step Two: Shuffle all cards together at least three times to randomize the deck.

Step Three: Place the cards facedown on the table. For younger children, or if memory skills are your primary concern, I recommend that you place the cards in an orderly grid pattern to facilitate short-term memory. For more advanced or older children, you can choose to scatter the cards facedown on the table.

Step Four: Player One selects one card from the grid and turns it faceup.
- He must name the person, object, or action pictured on the card.
- If he has found an object or action, he places the card facedown where he found it.
- If he has found a family member, he takes the card and gets the point.
    - Remember to celebrate the finding of a family member with a little cheer to reward his effort.

Step Five: Play continues clockwise (to the left) until all family members are found. The player who finds the most family members is the winner.

39. Link Up: Dominoes and Picture Cards

Target Skills: Categories, Parts of Speech, Shapes, Colors, Object Functions, Associations

Materials: Card decks for common objects (nouns: twenty-five), actions (verbs: twenty-five), shapes, colors, and sizes (twenty-five); parts of speech/phrase cards

Object of the Game: To build chains of pictured objects/actions/attributes based on a describable relationship. The first person to use all of the cards in his hand is the winner.

Step One: Use your child's knowledge to select the appropriate card decks for this game. Almost all of the card decks provided can be used, so choose those that will spark some imagination and creativity in establishing relationships between the pictured objects and actions. I recommend at least three different card types to allow a broad selection. You want to provide a variety and number enough so that all players can have five to seven cards to start the game.

Step Two: Shuffle the selected decks together well, at least three times. Deal each player a random set of five to seven cards. Caution players not to show their hand to other players.

Step Three: The remaining stack of cards is placed facedown in the center of the table. The top card is flipped faceup and placed where all players can see it to act as the starter card.
  • Example: The starter card is a **brown shoe**.

Step Four: The play moves clockwise (to the left) around the table with each player building on the resulting chain of cards.

A sample sequence:
- Player One places a **red sock** next to the **brown shoe** and says, "Because they are both worn on your foot."
- Player Two places a **tree** next to the **brown shoe** and says, "Because the tree's bark and the shoe are both brown."
- Player Three places a picture of a **red apple** next to the **red sock** and says, "Because both are red."
- Player Four places a picture of a **witch** next to the **red apple** and says, "Because a witch gave Snow White a poisoned apple."

Step Five: Players can build the chain based on any element, as long as they can describe a meaningful relationship between the pictured objects. If a player is unable to use a card from her hand, she must take a card from the deck. Play then moves to the next player.

Step Six: If the other players do not agree with the relationship described by a particular player, it is the adult's prerogative and responsibility to accept or rule out that play. If that turn is ruled out, the player returns the card to her hand and takes another card from the deck.

Step Seven: The first person to play all her cards is the winner.

40. The Laughing Joker

Target Skills: Matching Objects, Identifying Numerals, Counting, Strategic Thinking, Vocabulary, Card Playing Terms
- Holding Them Close to the Chest
- Keeping Your Eyes on Your Own Hand
- Not Showing Your Hand

Materials: You have several options:

- A deck of fifty cards composed of paired pictures of common objects, people at work, and/or familiar locations, plus one undesirable picture, such as a rotten tomato
    - For matching and labeling pictured objects
- A standard deck of fifty-two playing cards, including one joker card
    - For identifying numbers and counting
- A classic Old Maid deck
    - For adjective-noun relationships

Object of the Game: To survive game play to the end as players pair all the cards in their hands. The last player holding the joker/rotten tomato/old maid is the loser.

Step One: Identify the skill set you want to target for your child. This will determine the card deck you will select. The rules of play are the same for each game. You need a game deck that is composed of pairs of objects, people, or numbers, with one outlier card.

I will use the games The Laughing Joker/Old Boy and a standard deck of fifty-two cards for the purpose of providing clear play directions. Most households have at least one card deck somewhere in a drawer.

- Using a standard card deck, leave all fifty-two cards in the deck and add a joker (must have the same design on the reverse side) to be the Laughing Joker.
- You can also create an unpaired card by removing three jacks from the deck, leaving the jack of clubs to serve as the Old Boy!

Step Two: The dealer, usually the adult or a child in the group who has mastered the Riffle Shuffle (page 104) shuffles the deck of cards three to five times. With younger, less-dexterous children, use Smooshing (page 103) to randomize the deck.

Step Three: The dealer deals all the cards to the players, placing the cards facedown in front of each player, starting with Player One and working clockwise around the table until all cards are distributed evenly among the players. One or two players, depending on how many people are playing, may wind up with one more card than the others. This is fine, but you may have to assure the players that this does not mean they have the Laughing Joker or Old Boy.

Step Four: Instruct each player to pick up their cards, hiding them from the other players. This is an important skill in card play called "holding them close to the chest," a useful card-playing term that may require frequent reminders. The same goes for "keeping your eyes on your own hand."

Step Five: Being careful not to "show their hands," the players look at their cards and arrange them in pairs, matching colors (red and black), numbers (Ace = 1, to 10 = 10), and pictures (queen to queen, king to king, and jack to jack, if you are playing Laughing Joker).

Step Six: When all players signal that they are done arranging their hands, Player One puts down each pair from his hand, faceup on the table for all to see, retaining only those cards that are unpaired. Now it is Player Two's turn. The game proceeds clockwise around the group until all players have revealed the pairs from their hand.

Step Seven: Game play has now returned to Player One. Player One holds his cards fanned out and facedown to the player on his left (Player Two), who can see only the back of each card.

Step Eight: Player Two selects a card from Player One's hand and places it in her own hand without showing the card to anyone else. She now examines her cards to see if she can make a pair with the new card. If she can, she places the new pair on the table, faceup for all to see.

Step Nine: Play proceeds clockwise around the table, with Player Two offering her cards to Player Three, who checks for pairs, and so on, until the final pair has been made. You may need to remind the players of the three cardinal rules of card games:

- Hold Them Close to the Chest
- Keep Your Eyes on Your Own Hand
- Don't Show Your Hand

Step Ten: The player left holding the last card (in this case the joker) is the Laughing Joker.

Note: Take some time to talk to the players about how to develop a game strategy, and how to plan ahead based on the choices of other players.

- Hold the joker a little more obviously than the other cards in your hand.
- Try to fool the others by holding the joker as though you want to hide it.
- Place the joker in your hand in a place your friend has a habit of selecting (some people like to take the middle card each time).

41. M. Know It All

Target Skills: Categorization, Descriptive Vocabulary, Narrative Structure, Associations, Question Formulation, Sentence Structure

Materials: Object Noun Cards, one die. *Optional*: A searchable database or, preferably, an old-fashioned children's encyclopedia.

Object of the Game: To be able to describe up to six verifiable facts or associated concepts about an object/animal/person.

Step One: For younger children (ages three to six), select appropriate People/Places/Things cards from the Object Noun deck that are of common knowledge, of interest to your child, or that he is already familiar with. For older children (ages six to eight and up), you can broaden your selection to include People/Places/Things that are less familiar, such as historical figures or geographic locations he may have been exposed to at school. If you are playing with several children of varying ages, be sure to have a mix of topics of interest for each child. You will need twenty to fifty cards, enough so that play is varied and unpredictable.

Note: Go to www.simonandschuster.com/books/The-Gift-of -Gab to download companion cards for this book, and use the Object Noun Cards as a launching point for your family's creativity. Or feel free to develop your own card deck using photographs, pictures from magazines, interesting illustrations from children's books, or anything else that strikes your fancy. I suggest that you glue or tape these pictures to a standard deck of fifty-two cards so that the reverse side is less likely to give clues as to the face of the cards when you play.

Step Two: Shuffle the cards well at least three to five times (see the Riffle Shuffle, page 104, or Smooshing, page 103). Stack the cards in the center of the table.

Step Three: Player One takes the card at the top of the deck and flips it over so that all can see the picture. He then rolls the die. The number shown is the number of facts/concepts/descriptors he must provide about that person/place/thing to obtain the point.

- Example: Player One flips a card that reveals a picture of a firefighter.
  - His roll of the die lands on the number 6.
  - He must provide six facts/associated concepts about firefighters. For example:
    - A firefighter wears a helmet.
    - A firefighter puts out fires.
    - A firefighter can be a man or a woman.
    - A firefighter drives a big red fire truck to the fire.
    - A firefighter saves lives.
    - Firefighters and police officers are called first responders.

Step Four: If any player takes issue with any of the concepts or facts stated by Player One, the adult acts as the moderator and determines if the point is valid. With younger children, this may take the form of asking the child to explain his answer. If the explanation is logical within the child's experience, even if it is not actually accurate, you may choose to use the error as a teachable moment and, at your discretion, accept the point.

- Example: Player Two (age four) flips a picture of an elephant and rolls a 3 on the die. Her favorite movie is *Dumbo*.

- She must provide three facts about elephants. For example:
  - They are gray.
  - They eat peanuts.
  - They fly.

Given this example, you can choose to ask her to name an elephant that can fly. She will likely answer, "Dumbo." You can now explain that you understand her reasoning. While she is correct for the point, and Dumbo can fly, Dumbo is not a real elephant. Real elephants do not fly. Remember, you want to give your child the greatest language experience from each game interaction while maintaining her interest.

For older children, a searchable resource like a database or encyclopedia comes in handy.

- Example: Player Three (age eight) flips a picture of George Washington and rolls a 3 on the die. He learned about Washington in school when it was Presidents' Day.
  - He must provide three facts about George Washington. For example:
    - He was the first president.
    - He was a general.
    - He chopped down a cherry tree.

If you look up "George Washington and cherry tree," you will find that this is a common story about him, but it is not a verifiable fact.

"After young George Washington was given a hatchet, he used it to chop down his father's prized cherry tree. When his father asked who chopped down his cherry tree, George answered honestly. This story was used to show that George Washington never told a lie, but it's probably a legend."

As the adult moderator, you can then choose to accept the answer for the point, but now everyone knows the legendary nature of the story moving forward. This exercise has the added benefit of teaching the value of research and verification, an important skill for independence as children become mature students.

Step Five: Play continues clockwise (to the player's left) around the circle.

Step Six: The first player to gain seven points wins.

42. Bob's Birthday Party

This is a game that relies on a child's ability to use deductive reasoning. So gather your young Sherlock Holmes and Jane Marple crowd and have some mystery-solving fun.

Target Skills: Question Formulation, Declarative Sentences, Deductive Reasoning, Memory

Materials: Object Cards, Character Cards, Location Cards, an envelope. *Optional*: A notepad for each player.

Object of the Game: To determine Who gave the gift, What they gave, and Where they got the gift.

Step One: The dealer (adult) selects twice the number of cards as there are players from each deck type. For example, if there are four players, eight cards are selected from each deck type: Who (people), What (objects), and Where (locations). The dealer shows the selected cards to all players to establish a set of Who, What, and Where elements for the game.

Option: The players may choose to assist in selecting the Who, What, and Where cards, stating why they would choose each card. This is a great conversation starter with selections of desired gifts—gifts that are "white elephants." Why they would or would not shop in a certain place, and people they would want to invite to a party or avoid at all costs.

Step Two: The dealer shuffles each deck type (People, Location, Object) well at least three times. Without looking, the dealer selects one card from each deck and places it facedown in the envelope. The envelope is then closed and placed in the center of the table.

The envelope now contains Who is giving the gift, What they are giving, and Where they bought the gift.

Step Three: One more card is selected from the People deck and placed faceup next to the envelope. This is the receiver of the gift.

Step Four: The dealer shuffles the remaining cards from all three decks together at least three times. Each player is then dealt five cards. Now each player has five secret hints as to which cards are *not* in the envelope.

The remaining cards are placed in a stack in the center of the table, next to the envelope.

Step Five: Player One starts by asking any other player if she has one of the Objects, People, or Places. He must ask using a complete sentence ("Do you have the red sweater?").

That player must answer truthfully in a complete sentence ("Yes, I do have the red sweater"). If the answer is yes, that card goes faceup in the center of the table. If the answer is no ("No, I don't have the red sweater"), Player One must pick another card from the deck and place it in his hand, without showing the other players. Player One now has an additional clue, unknown to the other players.

Step Six: Play moves to the left (clockwise) around the table until one person feels able to guess Who gave What gift and Where they got it. The guesser must announce her conclusion to the other players in a complete sentence: "The Teacher gave a red sweater she bought at Walmart."

Only the guesser can then look at the cards that are in the envelope on the table. If she is correct, she places all the cards faceup on the table and wins the game. If she is incorrect on any of the three items, she returns the cards to the envelope. She then places the cards remaining from her hand faceup on the table. She is now out of the game.

Step Seven: The remaining players now have the benefit of all the guesser's clues. Play continues clockwise (to the left) until a player guesses all three of the items correctly.

43. Close It

A close sentence is one that has been intentionally left incomplete for the reader to "close" by providing words with a meaningfully correct grammatic structure. Sometimes called "open sentences," close sentences are the basis for many popular word games. Keep in mind that "meaningful" does not necessarily mean sensible. Laughs are encouraged! (When played by adults, these games can get a bit . . . risqué. Keep an eye on that tendency when playing with children. Even young children will go there.) It's up to the adult in the room to set the boundaries, but don't make the rules too rigid. Games are intentionally unpredictable.

Target Skills: Sentence Structure, Meaningful Responses, Grammatic Structure, Reading Aloud

Materials: Phrase Cards, Close Sentence Cards

Object of the Game: The players will provide a meaningful and grammatically correct word or phrase to complete a sentence.

Step One: Shuffle (see the Riffle Shuffle, page 104, or Smooshing, page 103) separately the Phrase Card and Close Sentence Card decks three to five times to randomize.

Step Two: Place both decks facedown in the center of the table.

Step Three: Beginning with Player One, moving clockwise (to the left) around the table, each player takes five cards from the Phrase Card stack.

Step Four: Player One takes the top card from the Close Sentence Card stack and places it faceup in the center of the table. Player One has the first opportunity to meaningfully complete the Close Sentence using a card from his hand with a grammatically correct phrase.

Step Five: Player One reads the entire sentence aloud to the group. If he can complete the sentence, he takes both the Phrase Card and the Close Sentence Card and places them facedown in front of him. He gets the point.

Step Six: If Player One cannot complete the sentence, he takes a card from the top of the Phrase Card stack, places it in his hand, and play moves clockwise to Player Two.

Step Seven: Player Two now takes a card from the top of the Close Sentence stack, repeating Steps Four and Five. Player Two now has an opportunity to complete either or both Close Sentences with an appropriate Phrase Card from her hand.

Step Eight: If Player Two cannot complete the sentence, she takes a card from the top of the Phrase Card stack, places it in her hand, and play moves clockwise to Player Three.

Step Nine: Play proceeds clockwise (to the left) around the circle. The first player to get five points is the winner.

44. Close It Challenge

Target Skills: Sentence Structure, Meaningful Responses, Grammar, Reading Aloud, Strategic Planning

Materials: Phrase Cards, Close Sentence Cards

Object of the Game: The players will provide a meaningful and grammatically correct word or phrase to complete a sentence.

Step One: Shuffle separately the Phrase Card and Close Sentence Card decks three to five times to randomize (see the Riffle Shuffle, page 104, or Smooshing, page 103).

Step Two: Place both decks facedown in the center of the table.

Step Three: Beginning with Player One, moving clockwise (to the left) around the table, each player takes five cards from the Phrase Card stack.

Step Four: Player One takes the top card from the Close Sentence Card stack and places it faceup in the center of the table.

Step Five: Player One reads the entire sentence aloud to the group. If she can complete the sentence, she takes both the Phrase Card and the Close Sentence Card and places them facedown in front of her. She gets the point. Play moves clockwise to Player Two.

Step Six: If Player One cannot complete the Close Sentence with a card from her hand, she challenges Player Two to complete the sentence. If Player Two can do it, he gets the point.

Player One takes a Phrase Card from the center of the table and adds it to her hand.

Step Seven: If Player Two cannot complete the sentence, he challenges Player Three to do it.

Play proceeds clockwise (to the left) around the circle with each player having an opportunity to complete the sentence. The first one to do it gets the point and takes both the Close Sentence Card and the Phrase Card as a point, placing them faceup in front of her.

Step Eight: It is now time to pick a new sentence to close. Play moves to Player Two, who now draws a new Close Sentence Card and reads it aloud. He has the first opportunity to complete the sentence. Play continues as in Steps Five, Six, and Seven until a player has successfully completed the Close Sentence. All incomplete Close Sentence Cards remain in the center of the table if none of the players can complete them in that round.

Step Nine: The first player to complete her selected Close Sentence now has the opportunity to complete as many of the remaining uncompleted Close Sentences as she can, using appropriate cards from her hand. If she is lucky, she can really clean up.

Step Ten: The first player to use all the Phrase Cards in her hand is the winner. You also have the option to continue playing until a player has accumulated ten points.

45. What Do You Know?

Some children find it difficult to answer questions. They will provide everything they know in a "knowledge dump" before they hit on the answer. This game will help clear up their confusion. The basic technique is to take the question form and invert it to create a declarative sentence. (If this description sounds familiar, it is because the basic skill of responding appropriately to a question remains the same as described in the game "Ask the Right Question and Get the Right Answer," page 91, but unlike that game this game does not focus exclusively on Wh-Questions.)

This book provides a list of twenty Trivia "Cards" (page 189) to get you started. Each of the Trivia Cards has six questions about a given topic, all selected so that most children ages four to eight should be successful. Use this format as a starting point to inspire your own cards for topics of interest to your child and family.

Example Topic: Flowers (with samples of appropriate responses)
- Name three types of flowers.
  - Three types of flowers are daisies, roses, and sunflowers.
- What are two things flowers need to grow?
  - Two things flowers need to grow are sunshine and water.
- What is your favorite flower?
  - My favorite flower is the tulip.
- Give two reasons that people like flowers.

- • People like flowers because they are pretty and smell good.
- • Is a flower an animal, a plant, or a mineral?
  - • A flower is a plant.
- • Name two professions in which people might grow flowers.
    - • Two people who might grow flowers are gardeners and farmers.

You will notice that there are no answers provided on the cards. This allows for a variety of answers to each question based on the child's knowledge level.

Target Skills: Categorization, Associations, Question Formulation, Declarative Sentence Structure

Materials: 20 Trivia Cards, one die. *Optional*: A searchable data source or, preferred, a children's encyclopedia in book form.

Object of the Game: Players will respond to various Wh-Question forms by formulating a complete declarative sentence correctly, providing the requested information.

Step One: Shuffle the Trivia Card deck well three to five times to randomize the cards.

Step Two: Player One rolls the die to identify the number of the question he must answer. He then takes a Trivia Card and reads the numbered question aloud for everyone to hear. If the child does not yet read, the adult can read the question for him.

Step Three: Player One answers the question using an appropriate declarative sentence that provides the requested information. If his information is correct, but his sentence form is ungrammatical, the adult moderator models the grammatically correct sentence for Player One to repeat. Player One gets the point.

Step Four: Play moves clockwise (to the left) around the table to Player Two. Player Two now rolls the die to identify a number and selects a Trivia Card from the top of the stack.

Step Five: If any player takes issue with any of the concepts or facts stated by another player, the adult acts as the moderator and determines if the point is valid. This may take the form of asking the child to explain his answer. If the explanation is logical within the child's experience, even if it is not actually accurate, you may choose to use the error as a teachable moment. At your discretion, you may accept the point. For older children, a searchable resource like a database or encyclopedia comes in handy. Treat all errors as teachable moments to keep all the children interested in playing the game.

Step Six: The first player to get ten points is the winner.

46. Tale Spinners

Target Skills: Speech Sound Production, Fluid Speech, Grammar, Verb Tenses

Materials: Phrase Cards (Adjective-Noun, Noun-Verb, Verb-Adverb, and Verb–Object Noun pairs), Story Starter Cards, Story Ending Cards (page 198). *Optional*: Close Sentence Cards.

Object of the Game: The players will practice their target speech sounds as they work together to create stories.

Step One: Select twelve Phrase Cards that incorporate the speech sound(s) you wish to practice with your child. For our example, we will use the context of s/t.

Select a variety of grammatic structures to make story creation more interesting, as follows:

- Three Adjective-Noun (less time, glass totem, nice table)
- Three Noun-Verb (mice took, boys ran, magician chanted)
- Three Verb-Noun (race time, eat cookies, sew buttons)
- Three Verb-Adverb (increase total, speak softly, dance gracefully)

Shuffle the cards well and place them in a stack in the center of the table.

Step Two: Player One selects a card from the selected Phrase Card stack and must clearly say the phrase. Any other player can challenge her to say the phrase three times before she is cleared to place the card faceup in the center of the table.

Once she has placed the card on the table, play moves clockwise to Player Two. Play proceeds until all the Phrase Cards have been turned faceup in the center for all to see.

Note: The adult moderator should limit correction of speech sound production to modeling the target phrases if a player mispronounces speech sounds. The object of the game is to complete the story. Refer to chapter 2, "Saying It," for guidance in the use of Modeling and the importance of Auditory Discrimination.

Step Three: Player One starts the story by selecting a Story Starter Card from the stack. She reads it aloud. Then she selects a Phrase Card from the group that is faceup in the center of the table.

- Story Starter: **On a day in the very distant future**, and Phrase Card: **Less time**
- Ex. 1: **On a day in the very distant future**, Bob will have **less time** than he thinks to steal the necklace from the museum.
- Ex. 2: **On a day in the very distant future**, Bobby had **less time** to get to school.

Step Four: The used cards are placed facedown in a stack to the side.

Step Five: Play proceeds clockwise around the table with each player selecting a Phrase Card to construct a sentence that takes the story forward, in any way they can. Any player can change the direction of the story or add characters, as long as they connect their addition to what came before.

- Ex. 1: **On a day in the very distant future**, Bob will have **less time** than he thinks to steal the necklace from the museum.
  - So he decided to steal the **glass totem** instead.
- Ex. 2: **On a day in the very distant future**, Bobby had **less time** to get to school.
  - Bobby had to beat his **race time** to get there.

Step Six: When only one Phrase Card remains, the next player selects a card at random from the Story Ending Card deck. She must bring the story to a satisfactory conclusion using that Story Ending and the last Phrase Card.

- He left the stolen necklace on the **nice table** and lived **Happily Ever After**.
- Bobby found the cheese that the **mice took**, and **the mystery was solved**.

Step Seven: Everyone wins when play ends with a completed story. Don't forget to celebrate.

47. Story Challenge

In this game, the added challenge comes in a player's ability to interrupt the story structure of other players, adding additional barriers to adapt around and create new story lines in the moment.

Target Skills: Speech Sound Production, Fluent Speech, Grammar

Materials: Fifty Phrase Cards (Adjective-Noun, Noun-Verb, Verb-Adverb, and Verb–Object Noun pairs), ten Story Starter Cards, five Story Ending Cards (page 198), Interrupt Cards, Pass the Buck Cards, Replace Cards. *Optional*: Fifty Close Sentence Cards.

Object of the Game: Players work together to keep the storytelling going until all cards are played. Phrase selection can, of course, continue to be made to target or avoid speech sounds as per your child's needs.

Step One: Select twelve Phrase Cards that incorporate the speech sound you wish to practice with your child. Select a variety of grammatic structures to make story creation more interesting.

- Three Adjective-Noun
- Three Noun-Verb
- Three Verb-Noun
- Three Verb-Adverb

Place the cards in a stack in the center of the table. Each player (up to four players) is dealt three Special Play Cards: one Interrupt Card, one Pass the Buck Card, and one Replace Card.

Step Two: Player One selects a card from the selected Phrase Card stack and must clearly say the phrase. Any other player can challenge him to say the phrase three times before he is cleared to place the card faceup in the center of the table.

Once he has placed the card on the table, play moves clockwise to Player Two. Play proceeds until all the Phrase Cards have been turned faceup in the center so all can see them.

Step Three: Player One starts the story by selecting a Story Starter Card and a Phrase Card from the center of the table.
- Story Starter Card: **On a day in the very distant future,** and Phrase Card: **Less time**
- Ex. 1: **On a day in the very distant future,** Bob will have **less time** than he thinks to steal the necklace from the museum.
- Ex. 2: **On a day in the very distant future,** Bobby had **less time** to get to school.

The used cards are placed facedown in a stack to the side.

Step Four: Play proceeds clockwise (to the left) around the table with each player selecting a Phrase Card to construct a sentence that takes the story forward, in any way they can.

Step Five: Any player can interrupt another player's turn by using a Special Play Card. The Special Play Card must be used before play proceeds to the next player. The interrupted player must change her story addition to comply with the command and still bring the story forward. If she cannot, she is out of the game and play proceeds to the next player.

Special Play Card Values

- **Interrupt Card:** Enables the player to interrupt the story line of another player and, using the same phrase, take the story in another direction.
- **Pass the Buck Card:** Enables the player to pass his turn to another player of his choice. The receiving player cannot use any other Special Play Card to avoid continuing the story. He must take the turn.
- **Replace Card:** Player Two can replace the phrase selected by Player One during Player One's turn with another phrase on the table. Player One must now continue the story using the new phrase.

When a Special Play Card has been used, it is placed face-down in the center of the table.

Step Six: When only one Phrase Card remains, the next player selects a card at random from the Story Ending Card deck. She must bring the story to a satisfactory conclusion using the Story Ending Card and the last Phrase Card.

- He put the necklace on the **nice table** and lived **Happily Ever After.**
- Bobby glued the nose on the **glass totem** and **the mystery was solved.**

48. Wizard's Wand

Rituals and chants are a time-honored feature of children's games. This game uses repetition of key phrases to support the language of polite interaction and cooperation along with introducing more academic language skills.

Target Skills: Asking and Answering Yes/No Questions, Categorization, Description, and Associations, Cooperation

Materials: Object Picture Cards, a stick or magical wand

Object of the Game: Using binary yes/no questions, the player (apprentice) must guess what object the wizard is holding to win the point and become a New Wizard. Play ends when all players have attained wizard-hood.

Step One: Select fifty cards from the deck of Object Picture Cards, one picture per object, no duplicates. Shuffle the deck three to five times to randomize the cards. Place the deck facedown in the center of the table.

Step Two: The adult game master plays the role of the Wise Wizard in the game. The other players (starting with Player One) are the apprentices.

　　The Wise Wizard picks up the magic wand, waves it over the card deck, and says the magic words:

- "Oh, Enchanted Deck, **please** show me a magical object to test my apprentice's skills."

The wizard takes the card from the top of the deck, looks at the card, holds it to his forehead, and says:

- "Thank You."

Step Three: The wizard takes the first eleven cards from the deck and shuffles them together with the "magical object."

Step Four: The wizard places the cards faceup on the table in four rows of three so that everyone can see all the cards, but only the Wise Wizard knows which card is the magic object.

Step Five: Starting with the First Apprentice (Player One) and proceeding clockwise around the table, the apprentices must each ask the wizard a question that can be answered yes or no. These questions can be based on a broad knowledge of categories and associations or specific attributes of the pictured items. There is one question per player until the play returns to the Wise Wizard. For example: There are five players and the magical object is a pencil.

- Is it alive?
    - I am sorry: No.
- Do you wear it?
    - I am sorry: No.
- Can you hold it in your hand?
    - I am happy to say: Yes.
- Is it made of metal?
    - I am sorry: No.
- Is it made of wood?
    - I am happy to say: Yes.

Step Six: The Wise Wizard waves his magic wand over the First Apprentice (Player One) and says:

> *"Apprentice, please tell me what is on my card."*

Step Seven: The First Apprentice (Player One) now can guess what is on the card. If he is not yet ready, he may request permission to ask just one more question.

> *Master, may I ask one more question?*

(The answer is always) *Yes.*

> *Can you write with it?*

I am happy to say: Yes.

Step Eight: The First Apprentice (Player One) must now guess the object on the card.

> *Please, is it a pencil?*

If he is correct, the Wise Wizard waves his magic wand over the apprentice and says, "You are correct. I have the pleasure of announcing to one and all that you are now a wizard. Please accept the Wand of Wizardry."

The Wise Wizard then hands the wand to the new wizard, who must say:

> *"Thank you, Master Wizard."*

Step Nine: If the apprentice is incorrect, the adult Wise Wizard may stop play to give him one hint. Keep in mind that you want every player to achieve the Wand of Wizardry, so you can make the hint as obvious as you want.
- "It has a rubber eraser on the end."
- "You use a pencil sharpener to give it a point."

Step Ten: Play proceeds from Steps Two through Five, with each apprentice becoming a New Wizard, having the opportunity to select a magic object, say the chants, and initiate another New Wizard. Play continues until all players have earned the Wand of Wizardry.

CARD GAMES FOR SPEECH SOUND PRODUCTION AND GRAMMAR

The parent skills that are described in chapter 2, "Saying It," are the most important ingredients of gamesmanship for speech games, if you are concerned about your child's speech sound development. When speech production issues do not interfere with intelligibility, or you just want to focus a bit on clarity, there are ways you can use customized card games to encourage the development of clear speech.

Keep it short and keep it simple by using single words or phrases of two to three words. You can select phrases that incorporate that specific troublesome sound. Or, if this is too distressing for your child, you can choose phrases that avoid those sounds altogether. The object of the exercise is to provide adult models of appropriate speech. You want to take the "sting" out of the act of speaking by making verbal communication less threatening.

Parents can also choose to select one type of grammatic phrase, such as Adjective-Noun, to encourage the practice of a desired sentence structure.

These games are tools you can use to design a format that addresses your child's needs and interests. As speech production improves, feel free to shuffle the card decks for a random selection of sound pairings and grammatic structures. The more proficient the child becomes, and the more challenging and complex the language, the more fun.

49. Talk Twisters

Target Skills: Speech Sound Production, Short-Term Memory, Rhythm and Rhyme

Materials: List of Sound-targeted Phrases, List of Sound-targeted Twisters, List of Classic Twisters, die. *Optional*: Create a card deck with one "twister" on each card, a container like a fish bowl or hat.

Object of the Game: The player must correctly say the selected phrase three times quickly to get the point.

Step One: Compile a list of phrases that include the speech sound you want to feature. The more syllables the words contain, the more challenging the phrase will be. These phrases do not need to be as complicated as the tongue twisters we are most familiar with. The important thing is that these should pose a challenge to the child, but not be impossible for him to say.

Sample Targeted Phrases for the /s/ Sound

p-s	The boy drank **grape soda**.
s-p	I would like a **nice pie**.
b-s	Go ahead and **grab some**.
s-b	Pooh is not a **fierce bear**.

See the Materials section for more sample targeted phrases for the sounds /s/, /r/, /l/, /k/, /g/, /ch/, /sh/, and /j/ (soft /g/).

Sample Targeted Twisters

- For /s/:
  - Small Store Sale
  - Sad Sam Said
- For /z/:
  - Zippity Zing
  - Zesty Zebras Zoom
- For /r/:
  - Random Rich Relatives
  - The Racing Rabbit Ran Rapidly
- For /l/:
  - The Lazy Leopard Lied
  - Loopy Lace Linen

See the Materials section for even more sound-targeted tongue twisters.

Sample Classic Twisters

- Pure Food for Pure Mules
- She Sells Seashells by the Seashore
  - *And the shells she sells by the seashore are seashells for sure.*
- Betty Botter bought a bit of butter.
  - *"But," she said, "this bit of butter's bitter."*

See the Materials section for more classic tongue twisters.

Step Two: Print each twister on a separate piece of paper. Two options to randomize the twisters:

- Fold the papers tightly and place them in a bowl or hat.
- Tape the papers to the playing sides of a standard deck of fifty-two playing cards and shuffle the deck three to five times.

Variations: You can opt to use a Cootie Catcher (page 82) to design a game with a limited number of up to eight twisters to encourage mastery of production or to simplify play for younger children.

You can use a single die to determine the number of times the twister must be produced to gain the game point.

Step Three: Player One selects a twister from the hat. He must clearly say the phrase three times to get the point.

Speed is not the primary point of the exercise; accuracy of pronunciation is the goal. You may opt to allow the child to say the twister three times slowly, or one time slowly with two fast tries. Identify a method that will be challenging but not defeating for your child.

Step Four: If the twister proves too challenging for Player One, other players may be given the option to take up the challenge for the point.

Step Five: If all players are unsuccessful in saying the twister three times, the paper is returned to the bowl or hat or placed at the bottom of the deck. The hat is shaken, or the deck is shuffled, to re-randomize the twisters.

Step Six: Play now moves clockwise to Player Two.

Step Seven: The first player to get five points is the winner.

50. Meany Meanings

Vocabulary demands become more complex once a child enters school and begins to read. Many words in English, as in any language, have more than one unrelated meaning. Comprehension relies on a child's ability to instantly recognize these words and their intended meaning within the context of a sentence.

This card game can be easily adapted to emphasize spelling skills for homonyms (words that sound the same but are spelled differently), depending on your intended focus. Mastery of vocabulary influences Reading Fluency, Auditory Comprehension, and Reading Comprehension.

Target Skills: Vocabulary of Multiple-Meaning Words, Grammar, Sentence Structure

Materials: List of multiple meanings of words in sentences, Open Phrase Cards, Word Cards. *Optional*: Create your own Word Cards and Fill-in-the-Blank Sentence Cards.

Object of the Game: The first player to correctly complete and explain five sentences wins.

Step One: Shuffle the Word Card deck three to five times. Shuffle the Open Phrase Card deck three to five times. Place the two decks in the center of the table.

Step Two: Player One flips over the top Open Phrase Card and places it faceup on the table for everyone to see. If he can, he reads it out loud or the adult can read the card for him.

- Example: If you _____ your _____ may fall off.

Step Three: Player One then selects the top card from the Word Card deck. He does not show it to the other players. If the word shown completes the phrase on the Open Phrase Card, he must say the sentence aloud and explain the two meanings of the word. If he does, he takes both the Word Card and the Phrase Card and gets the point.

- Example: If you <u>bow</u>, your <u>bow</u> may fall off.
  - <u>Bow</u> means to bend at the waist.
  - A <u>bow</u> is a fancy way to tie a ribbon.

See the Materials section for more multiple-meaning words and sentences.

If the Word Card does not complete the sentence, Player One keeps the Word Card in his hand and the Open Phrase Card remains faceup on the table. Play now moves clockwise to Player Two.

Step Four: Player Two flips over the top Open Phrase Card and selects the top Word Card. Player Two can now use his Word Card to correctly complete either of the exposed Open Phrase Cards for the point. If he cannot, he holds his Word Card in his hand and the Phrase Card remains faceup on the table. Play moves clockwise to Player Three.

Step Five: Play proceeds clockwise around the table. Each player has a new Word Card with each turn. Uncompleted Open Phrase Cards are available to any player to complete during his turn. The first player to complete five sentences to earn five points is the winner.

9. AT HOME AND ON THE ROAD

GAMES TO PLAY WHEREVER YOU GO

Look to your daily activities for inspiration in games creation. There are many materials you have in your home that you probably don't think of as playthings that will interest your child. If you use them, they will want to use them, too. If an item is around your house, you can find a way to use it.

Parents of small children often find challenges in the smallest daily chores when children are competing for their attention. With a little ingenuity you can mix game play into your busy life and make the day go a bit easier. If the kids go with you as you run errands, there's a way to take it on the road.

51. Pair Up

Even the most mundane chore can be exciting to a small child. Sorting the family laundry can be a fun game when you are just learning basic concepts.

Target Skills: Vocabulary (Colors, Sizes, Concepts of Same/ Different, Possession, Pattern), Visual Discrimination

Materials: Clean family laundry, laundry basket. *Optional*: A box or basket for each family member.

Object of the Game: Sorting the family socks, pajamas, and other paired clothing items.

Step One: The laundry is already randomized when it leaves the dryer. Explain to your child that she can be a great helper by looking for the things that go together.

Step Two: Depending on how much laundry you need to sort through, you can approach this in a couple of ways.

Select one pair of items, like socks (or a coordinated top and bottom set, popular for toddlers).

Then:

- Select two or three items from the laundry basket, one that matches your target, and the other one or two as "distractors." Place these items in front of her to choose from.

Or:

- Arrange all the laundry items on the table or clean floor so all are visible.

Step Three: Ask her to help you find the match. ("Where is the other one?")

Step Four: If she selects the wrong item, or she appears a little confused, give her some hints.

- "Hmmm, this sock is red. But that one is green. It does not match." (Then toss the green sock back into the basket.) "Let's find a red sock."
- Point out the most obvious feature of the item in terms of color, pattern, or size.
- Self-Talk and Parallel Talk are your most valuable skills. Use them!
  - "Where is the other big gray sock? Can you find it? Oh, you're right, that's gray, but that's a small

gray sock. This one is bigger. Can you find a big gray sock?" You get the idea.

Step Five: If she finds the right item to complete the pair, have a mini celebration. "Yay!" Congratulate your child when she finds the requested item. A little celebration goes a long way.

Step Six: Once she has found all the matching pairs, it's time for another game.

52. Who Does This Belong To?

Sorting games are great for any tidying-up chore like putting the clean laundry away or toy cleanup. This game is a natural companion to "Pair Up" (page 143). Make this game a part of the family's routine. Reward yourselves with a happy dance or a sing-along when you are done and all is put away. Not all rewards are edible.

Target Skills: Vocabulary (Colors, Sizes, Concepts of Same/ Different, Possession), Visual Discrimination, Making Choices

Materials: A plastic tub, laundry basket, or unique pillow-case for each family member, or you could just make a pile

Object of the Game: To sort all the items and stow them in the appropriate places.

Step One: Establish a pile, a pillowcase, or a different color basket for each family member. It can be useful to establish a color-coded sorting identifier for each family member that can be generalized to any sorting/cleanup activity. (Mom is red, Dad is yellow, Bobby is green, Baby is purple, etc.)

Step Two: Gather everything to be sorted into a pile on the floor or the table.

Step Three: Select an item from the pile. Ask him to identify the owner of the item.
- Young children can feel overwhelmed without set parameters to help organize their thinking. Feel free to give him choices.
  - "This is a big green shirt. Who does it belong to? Me or you?"
  - "Does this doll belong to Daddy or Gracie?"

Step Four: If he chooses the wrong person, give him more information.
- "I think it is too small for me. Let's see."
- "I know you like this shirt, but it is big for you. I think it fits me."
  - Try it on him and laugh at the result.

Step Five: Once you have determined ownership of an item, ask him to put it in the proper pile.
- "It's my shirt. Put it in the red basket," or "Put it in my pile."

Step Six: This activity can be a group activity involving every family member. You can set a timer for fifteen minutes to see if your family can correctly fill all the baskets and have everything put away before the timer goes off.

Step Seven: Remember to celebrate when you are all done.

53. Seek and Find

This game can be played anywhere. With a little preparation you can turn a trip to the grocery store, the main street shopping mall, the zoo, or a visit to Grandpa's house into an adventure.

Target Skills: Vocabulary (Colors, Size, and Shape), Following Directions, Reasoning Skills

Materials: Color, Size, and Shape Cards. *Optional*: A cell phone camera, voice recorder, or paper and pencil.

Object of the Game: Given five cards (color, shape, and size), the players must find an object that meets the specified criteria for each card. For example, something red or something round. The first player who gets all her points wins.

Step One: Gather all the shape, size, and color cards together to form one card deck. You may choose to engage the child(ren) in this step by letting them select the cards they want to include in the playing deck. This allows you the opportunity to review the vocabulary.

Step Two: Shuffle the deck well three to five times to randomize the cards.

Step Three: Deal the cards to each player. For younger players (ages three to four) you will need three cards for each. For older players, five cards total will do.

Step Four: As you travel to your destination, the players look along the road for things that meet their cards' criteria.

Examples:
- Red: A red stop sign = 1 point
- Triangle: A yield sign = 1 point
- Circle Railroad Crossing sign = 1 point
- Large: A moving truck = 1 point
- Green: Leaves = 1 point

Bonus points can be earned if the player finds an object that meets the criteria for more than one card.

Example:
- Red + Octagon: A red stop sign = 2 points
- Rectangle + Large + Yellow: A school bus = 3 points
- Small + White + Circle: A bumper sticker or business sign = 3 points
- Yellow + Rectangle + Large: A garbage truck = 3 points
- Medium + Brown: A chocolate Labrador retriever = 2 points

Step Five: When they see something, they must call it out to have another player verify the sighting. If this doesn't work for your crew, you can document the player's points by photographing their finds. This also allows for later discussion as to whether an object really met the criteria. Give the player an opportunity to defend his choice. His reasoning may surprise you.

The players can also have some fun by sharing the photographs with others when the game is done.

Step Six: As the adult game master, the decision to accept an object for the point or how many points to award rests with you. Be flexible. You can award bonus points for a "good try" or for a "creative explanation." Remember, your goal is to encourage participation and grow language through discussion.

54. Grocery Store Scavenger Hunt

Grocery shopping can be made into an adventure when you get children actively engaged. They can be helpful, too.

Target Skills: Vocabulary (colors, foods), Categorization, Same/Different, Compare/Contrast Reasoning

Materials: Food Picture Cards, two envelopes. *Optional*: Photographs of shopping list items.

Object of the Game: Your child will help complete the family shopping by finding items at the grocery store that match all the items on her list.

Step One: Before heading to the grocery store, look at the cards and select three to seven cards/items for your "scavenger hunt." To help you get your errand accomplished, select items that are on your family's real shopping list. Choose one item for your child's envelope card "list" from each department you will visit in the store (Produce, Meat, Seafood, Canned Goods, Breakfast Cereals, Paper Goods, etc.). This will keep her engaged and entertained for the entire trip. Put the cards in an envelope as her "Shopping List." Put the matching cards in another envelope for comparison at the end of the game.

Step Two: Take the opportunity to talk about your shopping list on the way to the grocery store. "Where will we find the yellow bananas? In the deli department or the produce department?" Don't be afraid to use "big" words. Real words are never too big for your child. Use the labels you would use when speaking to an adult. This is how a working vocabulary is built, one word at a time.

Step Three: When you arrive at the store, take the "Shopping List" cards out of her envelope. Review them with her.

Step Four: Work your way around the aisles as you would normally. As you enter each department, label it for your child and ask her to find a card from her list that can be found in that "department." "Okay, this is the produce department. Do we have to find anything here?"

Step Five: Once you have identified the item to be found, her task is to help you find it. "Can you see any yellow bananas?"

Step Six: When she finds an item, congratulate her. Now is also a good time to talk about what makes a good and healthful selection. "Those bananas are bruised. Let's find some without any brown spots." When you find a good choice, she gets to put it in the shopping cart and put the card together with its match in your envelope.

Step Seven: On to the next item. When you have completed your shopping, before you go to check out, look at the envelopes. Is her envelope empty? Does yours have all the pairs of cards? Yay! She wins!

55. Recipe Rangers

So much of a child's daily routine surrounds mealtime. Why not take advantage of his enthusiasm by pairing his love of food with language-learning skills? Planning his own lunch, making his own sandwich or mac and cheese will give him a feeling of independence that will last a lifetime. "I can do it!" starts here.

Target Skills: Value Judgment, Planning, Categorization, Compare/Contrast, Sharing

Materials: A simple recipe, a shopping list, Food Picture Cards. *Optional*: A trip to the grocery store.

Object of the Game: The player will determine what he needs to create a recipe, gather the ingredients, and prepare the meal.

Step One: Before heading to the grocery store or foraging through your kitchen cabinets, help your child select a simple recipe for lunch. For very young children it can be as simple as a peanut butter and jelly sandwich. It could also be one of his favorite foods, perhaps a grilled tuna melt sandwich.

Step Two: Ask him what he needs to make the "dish," including cooking equipment. For example, a peanut butter and jelly sandwich requires peanut butter, jelly, bread, a plate, and a knife or spoon.

Step Three: Together with him, select the cards from your Food Picture Card deck that represent what he will need to prepare the meal. Those cards are your "Shopping List."

Step Four: Using your "Shopping List" as a guide to start "shopping" your kitchen cupboards. You will probably find everything you need. If you have everything, skip to Step Six.

Step Five: Include the recipe cards for items you do not have at home in his "Shopping List" for your next visit to the grocery store when you play "Grocery Store Scavenger Hunt" (page 149).

While at the store, encourage him to select the necessary recipe ingredients, making value judgments and comparisons ("White bread or whole wheat? Crunchy peanut butter or smooth? Grape jelly or raspberry? Does your brother like grape jelly, too?").

Step Six: Now you have all your necessary tools and fixings on hand. Supervise him as he has the pleasure of using his cards to gather everything he needs (peanut butter, jelly, bread, plate, knife or spoon) and prepares his recipe for the meal.

Cutting sandwiches into shapes is fun, and a great way to introduce shape concepts like triangle, square, rectangle, etc.

56. Grocery Gambit

Target Skills: Vocabulary, Sorting, Categorization, Planning, Cooperation

Materials: Groceries, paper bags, kitchen cabinets, markers. *Optional*: Food storage containers.

Object of the Game: Working together, the family puts away the shopping within a specified period of time.

Step One: Once you have brought the groceries into the house, empty the bags onto the counter. Now is the time to get the child involved in sorting the items based on where the food is stored. Designate a space on the countertop or table for items that go:

- In the freezer
- In the refrigerator
- In the cereal cabinet
- In the drawer
- In his room
- In your room
- Etc.

There are as many ways to sort and categorize as there are families. Whatever works for you.

Step Two: If you have some personal items in with your shopping that need to be stored in a room other than the kitchen, you can take a marker to draw a quick picture or label a paper sack with the name of that space ("Bobby's Room").

Step Three: Remind everyone that this is a team effort. Your goal is to beat the clock, not each other.

Step Four: Set the timer. Start with a generous amount of time. Fifteen to twenty minutes should be enough time to begin with. Adjust the timer for your first time "playing" if you need to.

Step Five: Begin the sorting process. Your child may not know where everything goes at first. Ask leading questions to help her decide. Is it cold? Does it come in a box? A can? If the items need to go to another room in your home, she can put them in the paper sack for that room in order to carry them more easily.

Step Six: Once you have sorted the groceries together it is time to put everything away. The timer is ticking, so cooperation is important. Who can reach the freezer? Who can take the bag to Bobby's room? After a few times playing the game everyone will have settled into their role.

Step Seven: If your team has put the shopping away before the timer goes off, *you win!* If the timer goes off before your team is finished, mark how much more time you need to finish the task. This will become your "personal best" time to beat the next time you play.

57. Road Story

Long road trips can wear on everyone in the car. There are games you can play together to help the time pass enjoyably and grow language skills as you travel. This is a great game to play for trips that require a few stops along the way.

Target Skills: Descriptive Vocabulary, Noun/Verb/Objective Relationships, Narrative Storytelling

Materials: *Optional*: Storytelling Cards, Phrase Cards, Color Cards

Object of the Game: To keep the story going for as long as it takes to reach your first stop, using objects and people seen while on the road.

Step One: Since the recommended games to determine the identity of Player One are not possible in a car, establish who will be Player One before hitting the road. (See chapter 7, Who Goes First? for suggestions.)

Step Two: For safety reasons the role of adult game master is played by an adult passenger, not the driver. This, of course, allows the driver to do the most important job of getting everyone to their destination safely. The adult game master acts as game caller, starting the story off and then giving each player in turn a target word type, phrase, or object to incorporate into the story.

If materials such as cards or lists are uncomfortable for your family to use in a car or on a train, a review of the cards developed for the storytelling games in this book (see "Tale Spinners," page 128, and "Story Challenge," page 131) can serve as an inspiration for your directions. Another option is to tailor your directions to the skill levels of your child(ren) and the unique environment you are traveling through.

Sample Color Coding

- Nouns: Green
- Verbs: Red
- Adjectives: Yellow

Sample Road Story Starters

- Once upon a time in New Mexico there was a . . . (adjective-noun)
- The view from the train window was . . . (adjective)
- The man on Highway 10 was . . . (verb–object noun)
- (Child's name) saw a green lizard outside the window. What was it doing?
- This is the story of Dorothy Gale and her trip through Maine. Dorothy saw something out the window that reminded her of Oz. It was a . . . (noun–verb+ing)
- The name of this story is *Harry Potter and the* . . . (adjective–noun)

Step Three: Player One must complete the sentence with the required grammatic phrase. An older child can be expected to take the story line forward by one sentence using something or someone he is able to see. Younger children may be asked to find something that meets one or two criteria, such as something small and red.

Step Four: The adult game master sends the story line to Player Two. There may be a challenge in keeping one player from monopolizing the story (there is always one in the group) or keeping another player from yielding the story too often to other players from lack of confidence (another common player type).

Step Five: As adult game master, your job is to keep the story going. Change your directions to the players with the environment you travel through. Encourage all players to use their imagination. Introduce fantastic elements or incidents or characters from favorite stories. The sky is the limit.

Step Six: As you arrive at your destination, the adult game master, or the driver of the car, concludes the story with a story ender. Try to include your stop into the story or a person or thing you all can see.

Sample Road Story Enders

- They took the New Mexico magic charm into the <u>Red Lobster</u> and hid it in the lobster tank.
- The train pulled into the station just as <u>the man in the red shirt</u> finished his newspaper.
- The man in the green car waved goodbye as they pulled into <u>Grandma's driveway</u>.
- (Child's name) watched as the <u>green lizard</u> moved farther into the fog.
- The Scarecrow laughed as Dorothy's <u>boat</u> sailed away downriver.
- Harry and Ron decided that <u>the ice-cream parlor</u> on Main Street was the place to go.

58. Skippyroo Kangaroo I See Something, and You Do, Too

This is my own variation of a popular game played in many Australian preschools and kindergartens. The game is used to help children learn their classmates' names as well as develop good listening skills. I have emphasized listening for sound patterns and rhymes. You can play this game with a large group or one child. It's fun anytime, anywhere.

Target Skills: Rhythm and Rhyme, Sound Discrimination, Sound Patterns, Sharing, Turn-Taking

Materials: Nothing needed except you, your child(ren), and some imagination

Object of the Game: The player will use her knowledge of rhymes to identify a secret object in the room.

Step One: For group play, have the children sit in a circle. Ask Player One to crouch down with her eyes closed in the middle of the circle. She is now the Skippyroo Kangaroo.

Step Two: Player Two then looks around the room and finds an object for the Skippyroo to find. Player Two leaves the circle. He goes over to the object and silently points it out to the group so that everyone knows what Player One is to be looking for.

Step Three: Player Two rejoins the group. He must now think of a rhyming hint to give the Skippyroo Kangaroo (Player One) that rhymes with the name of the object she chose. The rhyme doesn't have to make sense. It is a clue for Player One to find the object.
  • The object is a **red chair = bed bear**
  • The object is a **big blue book = fig shoe hook**

Step Four: The other players now chant:
>*"Skippyroo Kangaroo, dozing in the sun,*
>*see a treat, and run, run, run!"*

Step Five: The players then sing the rhyme again, only this time Player Two ends the rhyme with his hint:
- Example: **red chair = bed bear**
  - All: "Skippyroo Kangaroo, dozing in the sun, see a treat, and . . ."
  - Player Two: "Find the **bed bear** just for fun!"

Step Six: Player One leaves the circle and searches the room for the object. The other players can give her hints when she gets close to the object by calling out hot, warm, or cold to let her know if she is getting closer. They can call out the rhyming hint "bed bear" to remind her that what she is looking for must rhyme with that phrase.

Step Seven: When Player One finds the correct object, she must call out the rhyme and the name of the object. In this example, "Bed bear, red chair!"

Step Eight: Everyone cheers to congratulate Player One. She now joins the circle and Player Two takes her place as the Skippyroo Kangaroo.

Step Nine: The game continues around the circle until all players have a turn to be the Skippyroo Kangaroo.

RAINY DAYS . . . SNOWY DAYS . . . AND OTHER STUCK-IN-THE-HOUSE DAYS

Stuck-in-the-house days can be a challenge for both child and parent. Once all the DVDs have been watched and the snacks eaten, long hours stretch before you. What to do? How about some creative role play? Here are two scenarios to get your inventive juices flowing. With a little imagination, you can enjoy the great outdoors together in your living room as a snowstorm rages outside your window. I have included mapmaking and reading in the skills learned in these scenarios. Even in an age of GPS and Google Maps, being able to decipher a two-dimensional representation of a three-dimensional plan is a required skill.

59. Rainy Day Beach Party

Target Skills: Planning, Vocabulary, Creating Maps, Fine and Gross Motor, Following Directions

Materials: Beachwear (bathing suits, large towels, sun hats, beach cover-ups, sunglasses, flip-flops, etc.), family vacation pictures, a road map or globe, picnic basket, snacks, drinks, a bathtub or plastic kiddy pool. *Optional*: A sandbox, a bright lamp (to simulate sunshine), patio string lights, crepe paper streamers.

Object of the Game: The child(ren) and parent(s) will work together to plan and enjoy their pretend trip to the beach.

Step One: Together with your child(ren), select the real-life location for your beach party. With younger children you can use your family album to spark their memory of a fun time they want to relive. Older children may enjoy taking this step a bit further by plotting their trip on a road map. If they have never been to a real beach, some pictures of tropical islands from the internet may inspire them to select a location.

Step Two: Once you have selected your imaginary vacation spot, locate the best place in the house for your beach or pool setup.

- If you are fortunate enough to have a playroom with a waterproof floor you may want to set up a plastic kiddy pool as your "ocean."

- If you don't have that option, the bathroom tub works fine.
- Once you have decided on the spot, set up your pool or decorate the bathtub with beach paraphernalia:
  - Brown or tan towels to sop up the splashes and simulate sand
  - Go as crazy-creative as you like when setting the scene. Add bright-colored crepe paper ribbons and patio string lights.
  - A beach umbrella
  - A music player (if you can, play ocean sounds instead of music)
  - Make it festive.

Step Three: Design a "road trip" course through your home for the family to travel through on their way to your beach location.

- Starting at the far end of your home, design your custom map to the "beach."
- Create a picture diagram.
  - "Turn right at the living room sofa and down the hall to make a left at the bathroom."
  - Remember to include places to "gas up" the car or stop for a snack.
    - Getting there is half the fun.

Step Four: Together with the child(ren) make a list of things you want to bring. Ask them questions. Let them decide what to take. Some of their suggestions may surprise you. You can assist their selection, but let them take the lead. Remind them that they will have to carry everything to the beach and then back "home."

- Pool towels
- Pail and shovel

- Books to read
- Drinks and treats

Step Five: Ask the child(ren) what they want to wear to the beach. See what they decide to wear. Here are some suggestions to make sure that everyone gets dressed in their best beach finery.

- Bathing suits
- Sun hats
- Flip-flops
- Sunglasses
- Don't forget the sunscreen. (Baby lotion will do the trick.)

Step Six: When everyone is dressed for the water, gather your things and hit the road. Follow the map you created in Step Three. When you arrive at your beach, relax in the "sun" and have some water fun!

60. Covered Camping

Target Skills: Planning, Vocabulary, Creating Maps, Fine and Gross Motor, Following Directions

Materials: Two high-backed chairs and a large sheet (to act as a makeshift tent) or a small camping tent; red, yellow, and orange tissue paper; a large bowl; a picnic blanket; sleeping bags; paper plates; plastic knives, forks, and spoons; sandwiches with the trimmings; chocolate and marshmallow cookies; a storybook or two; flashlights; a music player; stuffed animals

Object of the Game: The child(ren) and parent(s) will work together to plan and enjoy their pretend camping trip.

Step One: Select the location for your campsite. With younger children you can use your family picture album to spark their memory of a fun time they want to relive. Older children may enjoy taking this step a bit further by plotting their trip on a road map. If they have never been camping, some pictures of national or state parks from the internet may inspire them to select a location.

Step Two: Once you have selected your imaginary vacation spot, locate the best place in the house for your campsite setup.
- If you are fortunate enough to have a playroom, that's a good place for your forest.
- If you don't have that option, the living room, dining room, or kitchen work fine.
- A room that can be darkened by closing the drapes or shutters is a nice touch.
- Once you have decided on the spot, set up your forest:
  - Music player (if you can, play forest sounds instead of music)
  - Wooden chairs for trees
  - If you have any plastic flowers or leafy vines, these are terrific as scenery.
  - Two high-backed wooden chairs can serve as tent posts.
  - Have the child(ren) select stuffed animals from their toy box to populate the forest.
  - Place a large bowl in the center of the campsite. This will be your campfire.
    - Have the red, yellow, and orange tissue paper handy.

Step Three: Once you have selected your imaginary vacation spot, design a "road trip" course through your home for the family to travel through on their way to your campsite.

- Make your own custom set of directions through the house.
  - "Turn right at the living room sofa and down the hall to make a left at the bathroom."
- Remember to include places to "gas up" the car or stop for a snack.
- Use a picture diagram.
  - Have the children draw the map.
  - Getting there is half the fun.

Step Four: Together with the children, make a list of things you want to bring on your camping trip. You can assist by asking them questions or giving them choices, but let them decide what to take. Some of their ideas may surprise you. Remind them that they will have to carry everything to the campsite. If you bring it into the forest you must take it out with you.

- Sheet to use as a tent, or a small pop-up tent if you have one
- Sleeping bags or blanket and pillows
- Picnic blanket
- Paper plates; plastic knives, forks, and spoons
- Picnic basket or paper lunch bags filled with sandwiches, drinks, cookies, etc.
- Books to read (spooky stories, if your kids like them)
- Flashlights

Step Five: Ask the child(ren) what they want to wear while camping. See what they decide to wear. Here are some suggestions to make sure that everyone gets dressed in their best gear.

- Shorts or jeans
- Socks and sneakers
- Hats and jackets
- Sunglasses

- Don't forget the bug spray. (Baby lotion will do the trick.)

Step Six: When everyone is dressed for a camping adventure, gather your things and hit the road. Follow the map you created in Step Three. When you arrive at your campsite, set up camp.

- To pitch your tent place two high-backed chairs back-to-back, with enough space for the children to set up their towels or sleeping bags between the chairs. Drape the sheet over the backs of the two chairs to form a tent.
  - If you have a dining table handy, drape the sheet over the table for an instant tent.
- Arrange the sleeping bags or pillows and blanket inside the tent, along with the flashlights.
- Place a flashlight in the bottom of the large bowl you positioned in Step Two.
  - "Start" your campfire by crumpling the red, yellow, and orange tissue paper and placing the crumpled paper in the bowl. The light from the flashlight should glow nicely through the paper.
  - Or cut the tissue paper into strips. A small battery-operated fan placed in the bottom of the bowl will make the tissue paper strips flutter for a flame effect.
- Take your picnic basket or lunch bags and distribute the sandwiches, drinks, and snacks.
- Close the drapes and shut off the lights.
- Grab your flashlights and settle in to enjoy a spooky story while you eat.

10. LET'S PARTY!

GAMES FOR LARGER GROUPS OF ALL AGES

Entertaining large groups is always a creative challenge, especially if you are concerned about your child's speech, language, or social skills. Children's birthday parties, holiday picnics, or Sunday dinners can be overwhelming for some children. Call on your master-level knowledge of games when keeping children (and adults) entertained. There are games with cross-generational appeal that will keep your child involved, build relationships, and keep the conversations going for hours. Some are brain games; some are action games. All involve language, cooperation, competition, and fun.

61. Under the Dome

This makes a terrific birthday party game for very small children. Every player gets a little present.

Target Skills: Following Directions, Syllabification, Rhythm, Patterns

Materials: A large cooking pot or bowl; a small toy, a fruit slice, or a piece of candy

Object of the Game: Players will use their knowledge of syllables and rhythm to assist each other in finding a hidden object.

Step One: Select a piece of candy, apple slice, stuffed toy, or anything your child would consider a "treat." This is a Finders Keepers reward, and a reason to play the game. Get a pot from the kitchen cabinet large enough to hide the selected object.

Step Two: Ask the child who is "The Finder" to hide his eyes, or close them tight. You can also opt to use a blindfold.

Step Three: Place the selected object under the pot in a "hidden" location in the room.

Step Four: Call out, "Open your eyes and find the (treat)." Clap your hands in rhythm with the syllables. For example, the phrase "Open your eyes and find the apple under the dome" has thirteen syllables and so would have thirteen claps.

   "O-pen your eyes and find the ap-ple un-der the dome."

Clap-Clap Clap Clap Clap Clap Clap Clap-Clap Clap-Clap Clap Clap

Step Five: All players continue chanting, and clapping to, "Find the apple under the dome" as the child who is the Finder searches the room. Feel free to give clues. Chant softly if he is far from the dome, and louder when he gets closer.

Step Six: When the Finder locates the apple under the dome, he must tap the top of the pot in rhythm as he calls out, "I found the apple under the dome."

Step Seven: Play continues with another object and another Finder, until every player has had a minimum of one turn.

62. Show Time!

We seem to have lost our ability to entertain each other without resorting to screens. There was a time before technology took over our lives when everyone was encouraged to display a talent and have a little moment in the spotlight to entertain each other. I remember an interview with Ringo Starr of the Beatles relating how, in his childhood in wartime 1940s Liverpool, England, everyone had a "party piece" that they would perform at social gatherings. This is a great way to involve everyone in the family if you are seeking games or activities that will include child participants and encourage their language skills.

Poetry and practiced public-speaking presentations are often very helpful in situations where speech fluency is a concern. Orators and actors use the rhythm and tonality of practiced speech to hold audiences' interest. James Earl Jones (the voice of Darth Vader, among his successful stage and screen roles) is a self-described stutterer. When he is acting, he uses the rhythm and musicality of speech to successfully overcome his fluency challenges. My own students found that "singing" their speech in therapy sessions had the same effect.

Although this game is most appropriate for larger groups, it can be just as enjoyable for a small group of three or four people. You may choose to feature this game at a birthday party or family gathering where guests of all ages are invited to participate. The more the merrier. However, you may want to ask your guests to prepare a short song, poem, or anecdote to make the game enjoyable for all participants.

Remind everyone to encourage each other. Performing is hard for some people. If anyone heckles the performer, remind them that if they want their audience to cheer for them, they need to cheer for others. People who are mean-spirited will be asked to perform next. This is a great game for a backyard gathering, a picnic setting, or a campsite.

Target Skills: Memorization; Poetry, Prose, and Music; "Public" Speaking; Fluent Speech; Appropriate Audience Behavior

Materials: A ball, a stuffed toy, a magic wand, or other smallish object that can easily and safely be passed around the circle hand to hand; a blindfold. *Optional*: A music player, or if you have a talented musician in the family, a musical instrument.

Object of the Game: To allow each player to grow their public speaking skills as they showcase their talents through music or verbal performance.

Step One: Ask all players to prepare a "party piece." Some performers require a bit of preparation. Allow everyone enough time so that they are comfortable when called upon to present.

Step Two: Seat all players in a circle, leaving room for an ample performance space.

Step Three: Player One steps outside the circle and closes her eyes.

Step Four: Player Two picks up a small item, like a ball. When the adult moderator starts the music, Player Two passes the ball clockwise around the circle. As the music plays, the ball is passed from hand to hand around the circle in time to the music.

Step Five: At a time of her choosing, Player One calls out, "Stop!"

Step Six: The player holding the ball steps into the center of the circle and becomes the Performer. The other players should cheer encouragement to the Performer and help him to a successful effort.

Step Seven: Player One rejoins the circle and asks the Performer what he would like to do as his party piece.
- He can keep it simple and just say his name and his favorite subject at school or his favorite toy.
  - He can briefly explain why he likes it.
- He can sing a song,
  - and request that they sing along with him.
- He can recite a poem.
  - He can ask everyone to recite along with him to help him remember a story or poem.

Step Eight: At the conclusion of his performance, the Performer takes a bow while everyone applauds and cheers his efforts.

Step Nine: The Performer now steps out of the circle. He hides his eyes and turns his back to the group. The adult moderator starts the music.

Step Ten: Play continues with Steps Five through Nine. If a player has already performed, he passes the ball to a player who has not yet had an opportunity. Play continues until all players have performed at least once.

63. Captain, May I

Target Skills: Following Directions, Imitation, Cooperation, Abstract/Figurative Language

Materials: A large, open play space suitable for group play (more than three players, fewer than ten)

Object of the Game: The first player to reach the Captain and tap her on the shoulder wins.

Step One: First review with all players the "funny walks" that will be called for while playing the game. You can encourage the players to develop their own "dance steps" and the names they might want to give them, but here are some basics to get started. "Captain, May I" can be a lot of fun at family gatherings and picnics. It is a great way to encourage children and adults to interact and get some outdoor exercise. There are always some considerations when playing with a group that includes a wide range of ages, from very young children to grandparents. Be sure that all players are considerate of the physical abilities of others. They can help each other, too.

All steps can be taken forward or backward:

Giant Steps

- The player steps forward as far as his legs will stretch.
- Count steps: Right foot (one step). Left foot (second step).

Umbrella Steps

- The player puts one hand on her head and twirls as she steps.
- Count steps: One twirl = one step.

Ballet Steps

- The player comes up on his tippy-toes with hands clasped and arms joined in a circle above his head and twirls as he steps.
- Count steps: One twirl = one step.

Baby Steps

- The player places one foot in front of or in back of the other foot as closely as possible as he steps.
- Count steps: Right foot (one step). Left foot (second step).

Snail Steps

- The player moves as slowly as he can as he steps.
- Count steps: Right foot (one step). Left foot (second step).

Scissor Steps

- The player jumps while crossing and then uncrossing her feet as she steps.
- Count steps: Cross (one step). Uncross (second step).

Cartwheel Steps

- The player does a cartwheel.
- Count steps: One cartwheel = one step.

Bunny Steps

- The player hops.
- Count steps: One hop = one step.

Frog Steps

- The player gets down on all fours and jumps sideways.
- Count steps: One jump = one step.

Crab Steps

- The player gets down on all fours and moves sideways.
- Count steps: One movement of all four limbs = one step.

Step Two: Player One (the Captain) assigns each player a number.

Step Three: Player One (the Captain) takes a position at one end of the room or playground. The other players line up next to each other across from Player One, about ten to twenty feet (approximately four to seven meters) away. This forms the starting line. Each player should be far enough away from Player One for everyone to have room to move forward, but close enough to hear Player One's directions.

Step Four: The Captain looks around the room/playground/picnic area and identifies an object/person/animal. This is not shared with any other player, but can be shared with an observing adult, especially if the group is made up of young children. This is the secret word the others must figure out through their questions.
  - For our example the secret word is "squirrel."

Step Five: The Captain turns to face away from the line of players. She calls to a player by his number, at random or in number order.

Step Six: The player called upon must ask a yes/no question to get a hint about what the secret word is.
- Player Two asks, "Is it alive?"

Step Seven: If the answer to his question is yes:
- The Captain says, "Yes, it is alive."
  - Player Two then asks:
    - "Captain, May I take three steps forward?"
- The Captain can specify any type of step she chooses.
  - "You may take three (umbrella, baby, bunny, etc.) steps forward."

Step Eight: If the answer to Player Two's question is no:
- The Captain says, "No, it is not alive."
- Player Two stays in place.

Step Nine: If a player forgets to ask a question for a clue or forgets to say, "Captain, May I," he can be "punished" in two ways.
- The Captain says, "You forgot to say, 'May I' . . .
- . . . go back to the starting line."
- . . . take (up to three of any type) steps backward."

Step Ten: The first player to reach the Captain and tap her on the shoulder is the winner.
- This can be done by asking questions that are answerable by yes and taking steps forward until you reach the Captain.

Or:
- When his number is called, a player can, if he chooses, guess what the secret word is.
  - "Captain, is the secret word 'squirrel'?"
  - "Yes it is!"

If he is correct, he *runs* directly to the finish line and chases the Captain until he taps the Captain, like a game of tag.

Step Eleven: That player now becomes the New Captain, and play can begin again from Step Two.

If the answer is no, the player can receive a punishment from the Captain by being sent back to the starting line or taking up to three steps of any type backward.

Variations: The game can be played in other ways, depending on the needs and/or skills of your group.

For example: The Captain may give the players commands, such as taking two baby steps and two umbrella steps forward, to target following multistep directions.

- The player must respond by saying, "Captain, may I?" to which the Captain can say, "Yes, you may," and the player moves forward.

Or:

- The Captain can say, "No, you may not," and alters the command.
    - "No, you may not. You may take one umbrella step forward."

64. Alphabet Crunch

Alphabet Crunch uses a combination of formats familiar to daytime TV watchers. It's a trivia game that calls upon the child's knowledge of people, places, and things in their environment, their ability to write and spell for communication (perfect spelling is not a requirement) and their knowledge of the alphabet. It's fun for groups as large as a classroom full of students, as well as individual children on a rainy day at home. You might even introduce it at a family gathering or birthday party.

Target Skills: Categorization, Spelling, Handwriting, Alphabetization, Vocabulary Development

Materials: Paper and pencil for each player. *Optional*: Large books to act as visual barriers.

Object of the Game: Players will generate words starting with different letters belonging to six categories within a specific time limit.

Step One: Give each player a piece of paper and a pencil, pen, or crayon.

Step Two: Instruct the players to divide their paper into eight columns:
- Place the paper on the table as a wide rectangle.
- Fold the left-hand edge to the right-hand edge.
- Repeat three times.
  - This results in eight columns.

Step Three: Open and turn the paper to form a tall rectangle. Ask them to write their name in the column at the top.

Step Four: Announce to the group the six category names you have chosen for the game. Be as creative as you like, but be sure to use categories your players are familiar with.

Step Five: Ask the players to rotate their paper one turn to the left so that the folds form eight columns. Ask each player to write a category name at the top of each blank column with the word "Total" in the last column on the right.

Color	Flower	Animal	Fruit	TV Show	Movie	Total

Step Six: When everyone signals that they have prepared their game board, Player One starts the game by leading the group in singing the "Alphabet Song." At a time of his choosing before the song ends, he calls out, "STOP!" That is the letter for Step Seven. In our example the singing stopped at the letter *M*.

Step Seven: Player One establishes a firm time for everyone to be finished. He can set a timer or sing a song, but all must be done when time is up. Fifteen to thirty seconds should be about right. He can cue the group to "Go!"

Step Eight: All players start writing words that start with the consonant or vowel, in our example *M*, one word for each category.

Step Nine: When everyone is done, Player Two starts the game again, leading the group in singing the "Alphabet Song." When he calls, "Stop!" a new letter is identified. Just as in Step Eight, the group has the same set time to write one word starting with this letter for each category. In our example the singing stopped at *P*.

Step Ten: The game play now moves to Player Three, and continues as long as your group wants to, or for a maximum of twenty-six turns, one turn for each letter of the alphabet.

Step Eleven: Stop the game after five letters.

Step Twelve: Each player trades his paper with another player, who reviews the answers and awards the points. Caution your players to be as generous with others as they would wish others to be with them. Correct spelling is not necessary, unless you want to make spelling a focus of your skill building. In case of disagreement, the decision lies with the adult game master.

One point is given for each correct answer. In our example, the player (I admit, it was me) couldn't quickly come up with a TV show starting with *P*. The total awarded was eleven out of twelve possible points.

Color	Flower	Animal	Fruit	TV Show	Movie	Total
Maroon Pink	Marigold Pansy	Monkey Penguin	Melon Pineapple	Mr. Rogers ???	The Martian Penelope	11

Step Thirteen: A winner is defined as a person who was able to get all the points possible. So you can have multiple winners. Those who don't get all the possible points, like me, may learn something new as they are introduced to new objects and ideas.

65. And Then That Happened . . .

This is based on a timeless parlor game that is enjoyable for adults as well as children. I have used this game with groups of widely varying ages and it is always a lot of fun. You might try it at your next family gathering. It's a terrific way to encourage children to use their language skills after the dishes are cleared from the table or after dessert. This game is a rich conversation starter and is the launching point for sharing family stories about generations gone by. It takes a little bit of preparation, but it is worth it.

Target Skills: Grammar, Speech Sound Production, Narrative Structure

Materials: Paper and pencil for each player

Object of the Game: Players turn a family story into a surprising tale by providing key story elements without the benefit of context.

Step One: The game master needs to have a general idea of the story she wants the group to "tell" as the game progresses. This helps to create a story structure and to select the phrases the group will need in order to tell the story.

Don't share this idea with the group until after Step Three, after everyone has created the phrases they will add to the story.

- If you don't feel creative, use a children's book or short story as a template, replacing character and place names and the actions of the hero and heroine to reach their goal. The story can be as long or as complicated or as wild as your group.
    - Identify the following phrase types from the text that can be replaced by the players to change the story.
        - Adjective + Noun
        - Noun + Verb + ing
        - Verb + Object Noun
        - Verb + Adverb
        - Noun + Past-tense Verb
- Or, you can create your own story based on a shared experience.
    - Some story ideas:
        - How Grandpa met Grandma
        - Mommy's first job
        - What we did on our summer vacation
        - What happened when George cooked dinner
        - My trip to Florida

Step Two: If you choose an original story, write one or two paragraphs that establish the outline you will follow for your question sequence in Step Three.

Using our example: How Grandpa Met Grandma

Once upon a time, in the year <u>date</u>, there was a <u>adjective + man</u> named <u>Grandpa's first name</u>. One day he traveled to <u>place name proper noun</u> because he wanted to <u>verb + adverb</u>. The first thing he saw there was an <u>adjective + noun</u>. It did not interest him. It was different with the first person he met there. She was a <u>adjective + woman</u>. She interested him. He didn't know it yet, but her name was <u>Grandma's first name</u>. He was afraid to talk to her because he was wearing an old <u>adjective + article of clothing</u>. She was wearing a beautiful new <u>adjective + article of clothing</u>. He figured he would miss his chance to meet her if he waited any longer. He gathered his bravery, walked up to her, and said, "Pardon me, miss, but, <u>a compliment you could say to another person</u>." <u>Grandma's first name</u> laughed and said, "<u>Something you might say to a stranger</u>." Little did they know that they would have a future together. And it all started in <u>place name proper noun</u>, in the year <u>date</u>.

A story like "How Grandpa Met Grandma" can be a wonderful launching point for other family stories as Grandma and Grandpa share how they really met. Then Mom and Dad might share their story. Even in families where relationships are more complicated, there are happy stories to pass on as family lore.

A more fanciful example that follows the same pattern might read like this:

A <u>adjective + man</u> named <u>man's first name</u> met a <u>adjective + woman</u> named <u>woman's first name</u> at <u>place name</u>.

They decided <u>to make a Lego spaceship</u>. The first thing <u>man's first name</u> noticed was <u>woman's first name</u>'s <u>raspberry socks</u>. <u>Man's first name</u> wore a <u>blue Speedo swimsuit</u>. <u>Man's first name</u> said to <u>woman's first name</u>, "<u>I haven't seen a pretty girl like you</u> since <u>1992</u>." <u>Woman's first name</u> said, "<u>I don't talk to strangers</u>." And the others in <u>the place name</u> thought, "<u>Somehow, I think I saw this coming</u>."

Step Three: Create a sequence of questions for the players to answer that follow the structure of your story. Give guidance as to the type of phrase needed to build your story by specifying the parts of speech or phrase type you want. You can mislead your players as to the story they are telling.

- Sample structure for your original story of "How Grandpa Met Grandma"
  - Pick a year between 1990 and 2019: <u>date</u>
  - Adjective for man: <u>adjective + man</u>
  - Man's first name?: <u>Grandpa's first name</u>
  - Adjective for woman: <u>adjective + woman</u>
  - Woman's first name?: <u>Grandma's first name</u>
  - A place name: <u>proper noun</u>
  - Why do people travel to a faraway place?: to <u>verb + adverb</u>
  - The first thing they saw there was: <u>an adjective + noun</u>
  - What did he wear?: <u>an adjective + article of clothing</u>
  - What did she wear?: <u>an adjective + article of clothing</u>
  - The first thing he said to her was: <u>a compliment you could say to another person</u>
  - She responded by saying: <u>something you might say to a stranger</u>
  - What the world said: <u>a newspaper headline</u>

Step Four: Assign a question to each player. There are a few options for this step.

- Print out a copy of the list and give each player a piece of paper with one question to answer.
- Go around the circle and whisper a question in each player's ear.
- Place the questions in a hat and let each player pick one.

Step Five: Each player writes the answer to her question on a piece of paper and places the paper facedown on the table. The game master can assist young children who do not yet write by writing their response for them.

Step Six: The game master reads the story she has prepared. As she reaches each fill-in-the-blank section, the player who has that element reads it out loud to the group. Play continues until the story is ended.

MATERIALS

Please visit simonandschuster.com/books/The-Gift-of-Gab, where you will find the following materials to aid in your enjoyment of this book, including cards for the matching and memory games, and a list of conversational prompts targeted to your child's age and ability.

1. CARD HOLDER HEADBAND

A simple paper headband with a slot in the center to hold a playing card, and two slots, one on the top edge and one on the bottom edge about a half-inch from the end of the rectangle, to hold the paper in a circle.

2. PAPER DICE PATTERN

(Included in text)

3. COOTIE CATCHER

(Included in text)

4. ILLUSTRATED CARDS

Emotions (two of each)

- Sad
- Happy
- Grumpy
- Angry

- Worried
- Scared
- Surprised
- Excited

- Silly
- Bored
- Tired
- Proud

Clothing
(ask children to color in the pictures!)

- 2 Sweaters (Red and Green)
- 3 Shoes (Red, Green, Blue)
- 3 Rings (Diamond, Ruby, Gold)
- 2 Slacks (Blue and Red)
- 2 Shirts (Green and Yellow)
- 2 Pajamas (Polka dots for girls and Striped for boys)
- 2 Socks (Red and Yellow)
- 2 Underwear (Polka dots for girls and Striped for boys)
- 2 Hoodies (Red and Green)
- 2 Hats (Cap and Fedora)

Parent Animals and Baby Animals

- Dog/Puppy
- Cat/Kitten
- Chicken/Chick
- Frog/Tadpole
- Butterfly/Caterpillar

- Elephant/Calf
- Cow/Calf
- Horse/Foal
- Lion/Cub
- Pig/Piglet

Food (2 of each)

- Apples
- Pears
- Pineapples
- Bananas
- Ice-cream cones (chocolate and vanilla)
- Cookies (chocolate chip)
- PB&J sandwiches
- Glasses of milk
- Tacos
- Boxes of cereal
- Oranges
- Heads of lettuce
- Tomatoes
- Bags of potato chips
- Hamburgers

People (2 of each)

- Teachers
- Boys
- Girls
- Babies
- Police Officers
- Firefighters
- Doctors
- Veterinarians
- Shop Keepers
- Chefs

Places (2 of each)

- Grocery Store
- Department Store
- Home Kitchen
- Museum
- School
- Shoe Store
- Factory
- Train Station
- Airport

Shape, Size, and Color
(ask children to color in the shapes!)

1. Red
   - Large Square
   - Small Octagon
2. Blue
   - Large Circle
   - Small Square
3. Yellow
   - Large Triangle
   - Small Rectangle
4. Green
   - Large Rectangle
   - Small Triangle
5. Orange
   - Large Octagon
   - Small Circle

Some games require the following cards

- 4 Interrupt Cards
- 4 Pass the Buck Cards
- 4 Replace Cards
- Total 12
- Total number of pre-printed cards: 160

Choose Your Own Game Elements
(As referenced in chapter 8, A Full Deck)

- 4 Interrupt Cards
- 4 Pass the Buck Cards
- 4 Replace Cards

5. CLASSIC TONGUE TWISTERS

1. Pure Food for Pure Mules
2. She Sells Seashells by the Seashore
   - *And the shells she sells by the seashore are sea-shells for sure.*
3. Betty Botter bought a bit of butter.
   - *But," she said, "this bit of butter's bitter."*
4. I saw Susie sitting in a shoe shine shop.
   - *Where she shines, she sits, and where she sits, she shines.*
5. How much wood would a woodchuck chuck, if the wood-chuck could chuck wood?
6. Brave, bleeding boys battle bald, biting babies.
7. Through three cheese trees three free fleas flew.
8. Rubber Baby Buggy Bumpers
9. Red Bulb Blue Bulb—Red Bulb Blue Bulb—Red Bulb Blue Bulb
10. Freshly Fried Fat Flying Fish
11. Unique New York
12. Bobble, Bubble Bobble, Bubble Bobble
13. Pre-shrunk Shirts
14. Fish Shop Sauce
15. Toy Boats Float
16. Manly Men Munch Moose Mush
17. Blue Blooded Black Bugs
18. Randy Russel Rushed the Washing
19. Pink People Push Purple Paper
20. Two Park Pass, Four Park Pass

6. SOUND-TARGETED TONGUE TWISTERS

/s/
Small Store Sale
Sad Sam Said

/z/
Zippity Zing
Zesty Zebras Zoom

/r/
Random Rich Relatives
The Racing Rabbit Ran Rapidly

/l/
Lazy Leopard Lied
Loopy Lace Linen

/kw/
Quick Quiz Queen
Quack Quack

/k/
Corny Caped Cadet
Crispy Critters

/g/
Get Gum
Gary Gobbled Greek Grapes

/ch/
Cheap Chintz Chopsticks
Choosey Charlie Chose Chicken

/ s h /

Shape Shifter Showdown

Shady Shadow Chandelier

/ j / (soft / g /)

Genial Gentle Giant

Jerry Jumped Jauntily

/ t /

Terry Tasted Twinkies

Tiny Tomatoes Taste Terrific

/ d /

Don't Drop Double Drumsticks

Debbie Downer Does Dinky Doodles

7. TRIVIA QUESTIONS
APPROPRIATE TO AGES 4 TO 8

Flowers

- Name three types of flowers.
- What are two things flowers need to grow?
- What is your favorite flower?
- Give two reasons that people like flowers.
- Is a flower an animal, a plant, or a mineral?
- Name two professions where people might grow flowers.

Sports

- Name three team sports.
- What are two things you need to play baseball?

- Name two individual sports.
- Give two reasons why people should play sports.
- Is chess a sport or a game?
- Other than players, who else participates in a sporting game?

School

- Name three jobs (professions) that people have at a school.
- What are three subjects that you learn at school?
- Give two reasons a person should go to school.
- What is your favorite school subject? Why?
- At school, what is it called when kids take a break and go out to play?
- Who is your favorite teacher? Why?

Water

- Name two sports that are played in or on water.
- What do we call water that is in a solid form?
- What do we call water that is in the form of a gas?
- Name three animals that live in the water.
- Name three ways that you use water every day.
- Name three bodies of water you would find on a map of the world.

Eggs

- Name three types of animals that lay eggs.
- Name two ways to cook eggs.
- What type of animal lays the eggs you buy at the grocery store?
- What do you call the yellow, or orange, part of an egg?

- What is the hard, outside part of an egg called?
- Which lays an egg? The hen or the rooster?

Cats

- In the old saying . . . how many lives does a cat have?
- What do you call a baby cat?
- Which one is a cat: an ostrich . . . a lion . . . or a baboon?
- Describe a house cat in three words.
- In cartoons, what kind of animal is a cat always chasing?
- What sound does a cat make? Make it yourself.

Dogs

- In the old saying . . . who is a dog's best friend?
- What do you call a baby dog?
- Which one is not a dog: a huskie . . . a fox . . . or a dingo?
- Describe a pet dog in three words.
- In cartoons, what kind of animal is a dog always chasing?
- Name two famous dogs from books, movies, or TV.

Geography

- What town or city do you live in?
- What country do you live in?
- Is the state of Washington on the East Coast or the West Coast?
- Name a city you have never been to. Would you like to go there? Why or why not?
- Name three countries other than the United States.
- What are the names of the seven continents?

Fruit

- Name a red fruit, a yellow fruit, and a green fruit.
- Is a tomato a fruit or a vegetable?
- In what grocery store department do you find fruit?
- Name a fruit that comes in more than one color.
- Name two dishes you can cook using apples.
- What is your favorite fruit? Why?

American Inventors

- Alexander Graham Bell is credited with inventing this gadget that lets people talk to each other over great distances. What is his invention called?
- Who invented both the lightbulb and the first voice recorder?
- He didn't invent the automobile, but he invented the assembly line production that built them quickly and cheaply. What was his name?
- In what room of a house did Steve Jobs and Steve Wozniak build the first personal computer?
- What type of products did Madam C. J. Walker develop and successfully market?
- What famous 1940s movie star invented the technology that led to the cell phone?

Superheroes

- Name three superpowers that Superman has that no other superhero has.
- Who got his superpowers from a spider bite?
- Who is your favorite superhero? Give two reasons why.
- Which is the better hero, Captain America or Iron Man? Give two reasons why.

- Which superhero is better? Captain Marvel or Wonder Woman? Give two reasons why.
- If you could have any superpower, which would you choose and why?

Your Body

- Name the five senses.
- What is the largest organ in the human body?
- What organ pumps blood to all the other organs in the body?
- What are the names of the five fingers?
- What three things does your body need to live?
- Why should you wash your hands before and after eating or going to the bathroom?

Harry Potter

- What did Hermione Granger's parents do for a living?
- Who are Harry Potter's best friends?
- What would be the core of your magic wand? What would your magic wand be made of and why?
- How do you get sorted into your Hogwarts House?
- Was Severus Snape a bad guy or a good guy? Explain.
- What would your favorite Hogwarts class be? Defense Against the Dark Arts, Potions, Transfiguration, or Charms? Why?

Fairy-Tale Gals

- What made Rapunzel very special?
- How big was Thumbelina?
- What three things did the Fairy Godmother transform to send Cinderella to the ball?

- What did the Evil Witch give to Snow White to make her sleep?
- What did Cinderella leave behind at the ball?
- Who is braver? Alice Liddell or Dorothy Gale? Why?

Fairy-Tale Guys

- What did Aladdin rub to free the Genie?
- What did Pinocchio want more than anything else?
- In what storybook did Aladdin first appear?
- Peter Pan could never do this.
- What is the name of the boy who Pooh Bear and Eeyore played with?
- What is the name of Captain Jack Sparrow's pirate ship?

Clothing

- Name three things you might wear to play in the snow.
- Why is it called a pair of pants? Explain.
- Name three articles of clothing both girls and boys wear.
- Name three things you might wear to the beach.
- State three reasons people wear shoes.
- Name three ways clothing is fastened together. Which is the best way? Why?

Houses

- Name three things a kitchen is used for.
- Describe a mansion in three words.
- What are igloos and who builds them?
- What is a pitched roof, and why would you have one on your house?

- Name five rooms you want in your house, and why.
- What does it mean if you are "in the doghouse"?

On Vacation

- Which would you choose, City or Mountains? Explain.
- In what theme park would you find the Wizarding World of Harry Potter: Universal Studios or Disneyland?
- Name three rides at Disneyland/California Adventure.
- Which would you choose, Beach or National Park? Explain.
- How do you like to travel? Why?
- What three things would you take on your vacation?

Pets

- Do you have a pet? What kind? What is its name?
- Does a tiger make a good pet? Give three reasons.
- Which is the better pet, a cat or a dog? State why.
- Should you let your dog sleep on your bed? Give two reasons.
- Name five animals that are commonly kept as house pets.
- If you could have any pet animal what would it be, and why?

Family

- Do you have any brothers or sisters? What are their names and ages?
- What relation to you is your mother's or father's brother?

- What do you call your mother or father's mother?
- What is a cousin?
- What is one word for "brothers and sisters"?
- In three words, what does "family" mean to you?

8. MULTIPLE-MEANING WORDS IN SENTENCES

Two cards, one with a sentence and a blank space for the underlined word, and one for each of the following words: wound, produce, refuse, lead, desert, present, bass, dove, object, invalid, close, bow, bark, rose, right, mine, date, season, leaves, fall, squash, left, foil, type, and park.

1. The bandage was <u>wound</u> around the <u>wound</u>.
2. The farm was used to <u>produce</u> <u>produce</u>.
3. The dump was so full that it had to <u>refuse</u> more <u>refuse</u>.
4. He would <u>lead</u> if he could get the <u>lead</u> out.
5. The driver decided to <u>desert</u> his team in the <u>desert</u>.
6. Since there is no time like the <u>present</u>, to <u>present</u> the <u>present</u>.
7. A <u>bass</u> was painted on the <u>bass</u> drum.
8. The <u>dove</u> <u>dove</u> into the bushes.
9. I did not <u>object</u> to the <u>object</u>.
10. The insurance was <u>invalid</u> for the <u>invalid</u>.
11. They were too <u>close</u> to <u>close</u> the door.
12. If you <u>bow</u> your <u>bow</u> may fall off.
13. I taught my dog to <u>bark</u> at the <u>bark</u> on the tree.
14. She <u>rose</u> from her seat to accept the <u>rose</u> bouquet.
15. You were <u>right</u> to make a <u>right</u>-hand turn at the corner of the street.
16. That gold <u>mine</u> is <u>mine</u>!
17. She ate a <u>date</u> on her first <u>date</u>.
18. Fall is the <u>season</u> for pumpkin spice <u>season</u>.
19. He <u>leaves</u> when the <u>leaves</u> fall in the fall.
20. To make the casserole you must first <u>squash</u> the <u>squash</u>.
21. She <u>left</u> her <u>left</u> shoe at the gym.

22. He used aluminum <u>foil</u> to <u>foil</u> the alien invasion!
23. What <u>type</u> of computer do you <u>type</u> on?
24. There was no place to <u>park</u> the car at the <u>park</u> entrance.

9. GETTING TO KNOW YOU QUESTIONS, WITH FOLLOW-UP QUESTIONS, APPROPRIATE FOR YOUNG CHILDREN

1. What is your favorite toy?
   - Why is it your favorite?
   - Who gave it to you?
2. What town do you live in?
   - What is the name of the street you live on?
   - What park do you think is the best to play in?
3. Who is your favorite superhero?
   - If you could have a superpower, what would it be?
   - Why is that superpower the best?
4. How would you describe yourself with only one word?
5. When do you wear pajamas, other than bedtime?
   - What color are your favorite pajamas?
   - Do you have a favorite blanket?
6. If you could call only one person, who would you call?
7. Who is the best cook in your family?
   - What do they cook that is the best?
8. What are you good at that your parents are good at, too?
9. Where in the world do you most want to go?
   - What do you want to see there?
   - How would you get there?
10. Do you have any pets?
    - What kind of pet(s)?
    - What are their names?
11. How many brothers and/or sisters do you have?
    - What are their names?
    - Who is the oldest? Who is the youngest?

12. What is your middle name?
    • What is your last name?
13. Who is your favorite TV character?
    • What is the name of the show he/she is on?
    • Name one more character from the show.
14. What celebrity would you like to meet someday?
    • Why are they famous?
15. What is your best talent?
    • Do you take lessons?
    • Do you want to take lessons?

10. FIVE STORY STARTERS: ONE CARD FOR EACH STARTER

1. Once Upon a Time
2. Many Long Years Ago
3. On a Day in the Very Distant Future
4. On a Dark and Stormy Night
5. Just Yesterday I Found Out That

11. FIVE STORY ENDINGS: ONE CARD FOR EACH ENDING

1. . . . and that is how it all ended.
2. . . . or so they say.
3. . . . but that is a story for another day.
4. . . . and they lived happily ever after.
5. . . . so, the mystery was solved.

12. PARTS OF SPEECH:
SAMPLE PHRASES AND SENTENCES

Put on your creative thinking caps and charge them up! To get you started, here are Sample Phrases along with Sample Mix-and-Match Close Sentences marking the parts of speech needed to complete them. Add your own phrases and sentences to the lists.

Twenty Adjective + Noun Phrases

- Bashful boy
- Friendly puppy
- Goofy cat
- Nice day
- Gloomy Gus
- Pretty dress
- New shoes
- Soft blanket
- Creative hobby
- Great gobs
- Graceful dancer
- Famous detective
- Classical music
- Rock star
- Favorite teacher
- Good news
- Big city
- Small town
- Chapter book
- Grape soda

Fifteen "Is + Verb + ing" Phrases

- is walking
- is eating
- is growing
- is coming
- is crying
- is wearing
- is dancing
- is finding
- is playing
- is drinking
- is sleeping
- is teaching
- is friendly
- is reading
- is cooking

Ten Verb + Object Noun Phrases

- Cook food
- Sew costumes
- Paint pictures
- Walk dogs
- Eat sausages
- Love stories
- Fold clothes
- Sort laundry
- Wear socks
- Cut paper

Five Verb + Adverb Phrases

- Cook slowly
- Speak softly
- Sing loudly
- Dance spritely
- Write quickly

Ten Sample Mix-and-Match Close Sentences with Sample Responses

1. The <u>Adjective + Noun</u> wanted to live in a <u>Adjective + Noun</u> so that he could become a <u>Adjective + Noun</u> and <u>Verb + Object Noun</u>.
   - The <u>bashful boy</u> wanted to live in a <u>big city</u> so he could become a <u>famous detective</u> and <u>paint pictures</u>.
2. Once upon a time there was a <u>Adjective + Noun</u> who could <u>Verb + Object Noun</u> but could not <u>Verb + Object Noun</u>.
   - Once upon a time there was a <u>gloomy Gus</u> who could <u>sort laundry</u> but could not <u>fold clothes</u>.
3. By the end of this lesson the <u>Adjective + Noun</u> will learn to <u>Verb + Object Noun</u> and <u>Verb + Adverb</u>.
   - By the end of this lesson the <u>bashful boy</u> will learn to <u>love stories</u> and <u>write quickly</u>.
4. The <u>Adjective + Noun</u> will <u>Verb + Adverb</u> and the <u>Adjective + Noun</u> will <u>Verb + Adverb</u> for your listening pleasure.
   - The <u>goofy cat</u> will <u>dance spritely</u> and the <u>friendly dog</u> will <u>sing loudly</u> for your listening pleasure.
5. Nobody will <u>Verb + Object Noun</u> until the <u>Adjective + Noun</u> has <u>Verb + Object Noun</u>.
   - Nobody will <u>eat sausages</u> until the <u>famous chef</u> has <u>cooked potatoes</u>.
6. You must learn to <u>Verb + Adverb</u> if you are going to be a <u>Adjective + Noun</u>.

- You must learn to <u>sing loudly</u> if you are going to be a <u>rock star</u>.
7. We will all <u>Verb + Object Noun</u> while the <u>Adjective + Noun</u> is <u>Verb+ing</u>.
   - We will all <u>sew costumes</u> while the <u>graceful dancer</u> is <u>sleeping</u>.
8. My mother said to <u>Verb + Adverb</u> as we <u>Verb + Object Noun</u>.
   - My mother said to <u>speak softly</u> as we <u>cut paper</u>.
9. His <u>Adjective + Noun</u> is <u>Verb+ing</u> a <u>Adjective + Noun</u> to the <u>Adjective + Noun</u>.
   - His <u>favorite teacher</u> is <u>reading</u> a <u>chapter book</u> to the <u>rock star</u>.
10. The <u>Adjective + Noun</u> will <u>Verb + Object Noun</u> for the <u>Adjective + Noun</u>.
    - The <u>bashful boy</u> will <u>cook food</u> for the <u>friendly puppy</u>.

13. THE EIGHT MOST FREQUENTLY MISARTICULATED SOUNDS IN CONTEXTS WITH PHRASES AND SENTENCES

Below are Sample Phrases for the eight most frequently misarticulated sounds in the various consonant/consonant contexts. I have provided Sample Phrases along with Close Sentences to get you started. Don't be afraid to use unfamiliar words. Kids love new vocabulary. Be creative, and maybe even a little silly, as you create your own phrases and sentences. That is what makes playing fun.

/S/

p-s	The boy drank **grape soda.**
s-p	I would like a **nice pie.**
b-s	Go ahead and **grab some.**
s-b	Pooh is not a **fierce bear.**

t-s	Blow on the **hot soup.**
s-t	When is the next **race time?**
d-s	He had a **good son.**
s-d	The baker made **less dough.**
k-s	Look for the **pink sand.**
s-k	My mother is a **famous cook.**
g-s	I am a **big sister.**
s-g	The fence has a **loose gate.**
m-s	I would like a **lime soda.**
s-m	This recipe uses **less milk.**
n-s	I can't find my **clean sock.**
s-n	The fish escaped the **loose net.**
f-s	I like the song that the **chef sang.**
s-f	He lost what his **boss found.**
v-s	I made cookies. Please **have some.**
s-v	He broke the **glass vase.**
th-s	I went **with Sam.**
s-th	I don't know what my **niece thought.**
sh-s	Mom bought **fresh sole.**
s-sh	Is that **cactus sharp?**
ch-s	Grandpa was a **Dutch sailor.**
s-ch	The actor has a **famous chin.**
j-s	The brewer taught me how to **age cider.**
s-j	I fell when the **horse jerked.**
l-s	Every night the coyote would **howl sadly.**
s-l	I want a dress with **less lace.**
r-s	We are very proud of **our son.**
s-r	What you need is a **nice rest.**
s-y	This bread needs **less yeast.**

/R/

p-r	He ate a **ripe radish**.
r-p	Please, I want **more pie**.
b-r	The scientist is a **lab rat**.
r-b	She has **four books**.
t-r	That is **not right**.
r-t	He needs **more time**.
d-r	Bugs is a **bad rabbit**.
r-d	We love **our dad**.
k-r	Mommy has a **pink robe**.
r-k	I **adore candy**.
g-r	Yikes! I see a **big rat**!
r-g	Movie stars often **wear gowns**.
m-r	The tires have **chrome rims**.
r-m	I want **more money**!
n-r	That is a **fine ring**.
r-n	I can **hear Nancy**.
f-r	The horse was a **safe ride**.
r-f	Next time it will be even **more fun**.
v-r	With your dinner you can **have rice**.
r-v	We had a **clear view**.
th-r	Stop arguing! You are **both right**!
r-th	Give your answer **more thought**.
sh-r	Did you **finish reading**?
r-sh	The cookie dough needs **more sugar**.
ch-r	Please, I want my sandwich on a **French roll**.
r-ch	He is **our champion**.
j-r	Dad wears a **beige robe**.
r-j	The ring had **four jewels**.
l-r	He gave his mother a **small rose**.
r-l	Mary had **four lambs**.
s-r	In the lion pride the **lioness ruled**.

| r-s | For a better salad, use **better celery**. |
| r-y | He made a **louder yell!** |

/L/

p-l	We made the lemonade with **ripe lemons**.
l-p	Her dress was **all purple**.
b-l	He drove in the **cab lane**.
l-b	I don't know which shirt he **will buy**.
t-l	Sally will **date Larry**.
l-t	It opens with a **pull tab**.
d-l	He exclaimed, "**Good Lord!**"
l-d	Does the pet store **sell ducks?**
k-l	The house is on a **brick lane**.
l-k	Did he say when he **will call?**
g-l	She learned a **big lesson**.
l-g	This is a job for a **tall girl**.
m-l	The Joker is a **crime lord**.
l-m	These clothes are for **tall men**.
n-l	The wedding gown was made of **fine lace**.
l-n	He stayed up **all night**.
f-l	The drink was half lime, **half lemon**.
l-f	Do you know how to **grill fish?**
v-l	The scientist wants to **save lions**.
l-v	That sounds like a **cool vacation**.
th-l	Choose something you **both like**.
l-th	That is a **terrible thought!**
sh-l	I won the **cash lottery!**
l-sh	He is **all show**.
ch-l	Grandma is a **church lady**.
l-ch	They sat on **pearl chairs**.
j-l	Jack climbed a **huge ladder**.

l-j	He fought the **cruel giant**.
l-r	How fast can a **camel run**?
r-l	I want to hear **more laughter**.
s-l	When does the **bus leave**?
l-s	If we don't watch him, the baby will **spill cereal**.
l-y	He told Santa that he was good **all year**.

/K/

p-k	When we go to the movies, we always **eat popcorn**.
k-p	I like to watch the **duck paddle**.
b-k	A mountain lion is different from **a bobcat**.
k-b	We will take a taxi to Grandma's and then **walk back**.
t-k	My dad bakes **great cakes**.
k-t	Englishmen like to **drink tea**.
d-k	Tricksy is a **bad cat**.
k-d	He gave her a **fake diamond**.
k-r	We won the **sack race**!
r-k	I always want **more candy**.
k-g	We planted a **sidewalk garden**.
m-k	That is the **same kid**.
k-m	You can't **make me**.
n-k	She wore a **fine cape**.
k-n	The actor always used a **fake knife**.
f-k	When the mother cow mooed, the **calf came**.
k-f	The peas were **quick frozen**.
v-k	The mother cat had **five kittens**.
k-v	His robe was made of **thick velvet**.
th-k	Do it **with kindness**.
k-th	Be careful not to **break them**!

sh-k	For breakfast we had **fresh kippers.**
k-st	My grandpa tells a **terrific story.**
ch-k	A babysitter is paid to **watch kids.**
k-ch	Most Holy Trinity is a **brick church.**
j-k	**cage creatures**
k-j	**speak gently**
l-k	My grandma likes a **full kitchen.**
k-l	He took out a **bank loan.**
s-k	Just do what the **book says.**
k-s	Our cabin is on the **lake side.**
k-y	Always say please and **thank you.**

/G/

p-g	She gave him a **cheap gift.**
g-p	I baked a **big pie.**
b-g	To make meat tasty, just **rub garlic.**
g-b	He is a **big boy.**
t-g	The movie is about to **get good.**
g-t	The Broadway show was really **big time!**
d-g	My dog is a **bad girl.**
g-d	It was a really **big deal!**
k-g	We played a **chess game.**
g-k	I like the chicken that **Doug cooked.**
g-r	We all watched as the **dog ran.**
r-g	King Midas wanted **more gold.**
m-g	They both gave him the **same gift.**
g-m	They called their grandmother **Big Momma.**
n-g	All of her jewelry was made of **fine gold.**
g-n	The fox stole all the hen's eggs. He was an **egg-napper.**
f-g	We made a **safe getaway.**

g-f	The peacock's tail has a **big feather**.
v-g	This story is about a **brave goose**.
g-v	The Joker is a **smug villain**.
th-g	I always cook **with garlic**.
g-th	The giant sewed using a **big thimble**.
sh-g	The mansion had a **lush garden**.
g-sh	That is the fence that the huge **pig shook**.
ch-g	On Sundays my family likes to **watch games**.
g-ch	They got married in a **big church**.
j-g	The zoo refused to **cage gorillas**.
g-j	How many balls can **Doug juggle**?
l-g	The school had no boys. It was **all girls**.
g-l	She sold dried fruit so we called her the **Fig Lady**.
s-g	Give your engine **less gas**.
g-s	He is the little brother and I am the **big sister**.
g-y	The sailor knows how to **rig yachts**.

/CH/

p-ch	The pie was made with **ripe cherries**.
ch-p	I don't know any **rich people**.
b-ch	Is that the lettuce that **Bob chopped**?
ch-b	Dorothy took the **witch broom**
t-ch	Would you like some **hot chocolate**?
ch-t	He climbed the **Dutch tower**.
d-ch	There is no such thing as **bad cheesecake**.
ch-d	When will we **reach Denver**?
k-ch	He sat on a **weak chair**.
ch-k	Richie Rich is a **rich kid**.
g-ch	You ain't nothin' but a **big chicken**.

ch-g	The groundskeeper's job was to lock windows and **latch gates**.
m-ch	Tune in next week on this **same channel**.
ch-m	My grandpa fixes watches so we call him the **Watch Man**.
n-ch	On her neck she wore a **thin chain**.
ch-n	The juggler used his hat to **catch knives**.
f-ch	The meatballs are half beef and **half chicken**.
ch-f	He was frightened when the **witch flew**.
v-ch	The robber ran, and the policeman **gave chase**.
ch-v	When will we **reach Vegas**?
th-ch	She loved **both children**.
ch-th	When you get your lottery tickets, **scratch them**.
sh-ch	We waited for the priest to **finish chanting**.
ch-sh	Forest Gump bought a boat to **catch shrimp**.
ch-r	When will we **reach Rome**?
r-ch	My favorite soap opera is called *All Our Children*.
j-ch	The wicked wizard planned to **cage children**.
ch-j	The policeman waited to **catch jaywalkers**.
l-ch	I won't play with Paul because **Paul cheats**.
ch-l	The littlest chick will **hatch last**.
s-ch	Shirley Temple was a **famous child**.
ch-s	Onions are used in a **French soup**.
ch-y	Van Gogh painted his flowers with a **rich yellow**.

/SH/

p-sh	Put it on the **top shelf**.
sh-p	The proud baker only sold **fresh pies**.
b-sh	When they caught the thief the **mob shouted**.
sh-b	The zookeeper's job was to **wash bears**.
t-sh	If anyone should, **Kate should**.
sh-t	For this recipe you will need **fresh thyme**.
d-sh	Give the butter churn a **good shake**.
sh-d	If you want to buy the house you must put **cash down**.
k-sh	The carwash promised to give your car a **quick shine**.
sh-k	Put it in the **trash can**.
g-sh	The clown wore **big shoes**.
sh-g	We all looked for Nemo. Where has that **fish gone**?
m-sh	We all wore the **same shoes**.
sh-m	His name is Aquaman, not **Fish Man**!
n-sh	She was cold because all she had was a **thin shawl**.
sh-n	Did I ever tell you about my **foolish neighbor**?
f-sh	The knight fought with a **tough shield**.
sh-f	What will you **wish for**?
v-sh	Barnum was a **brave showman**.
sh-v	The poet wanted to **publish verses**.
th-sh	Polish them and make them **both shiny**.
sh-th	To get them clean you must **wash them**.
sh-r	When I clean the dishes, I use **wash rags**.
r-sh	We want to watch **our show**.
ch-sh	Do you know which foot goes with **which shoe**?

sh-ch	To make a big mess, I would **crush chalk**.
j-sh	Water will **damage shoes**.
sh-j	To make his green paint, Michelangelo would **crush jade**.
l-sh	Which color **will shine** the brightest?
sh-l	The spaceship made a **crash landing**.
s-sh	If you are on a diet, make your cookie recipe with **less sugar**.
sh-s	Nothing tastes better than a **fresh salad**.
sh-y	Dad did all the **wash yesterday**.

/J/ (Soft G)

p-j	The Chief Justice is the **top judge**.
j-p	It is a good idea to **change pants**.
b-j	I spilled my coffee when the **cab jerked**.
j-b	If the wine is not corked right it will **age badly**.
t-j	I **hate Jell-O**!
j-t	It is not easy to **budge tigers**.
d-j	When it comes to poetry, he is a **bad judge**.
j-d	He is on an **orange diet**.
k-j	Onyx is a **black gem**.
j-k	People like houses with **large kitchens**.
g-j	He thinks he is a **big joker**.
j-g	Do not **enrage goats**!
m-j	When we are confused my whole family makes the **same gesture**.
j-m	Don't even try to **change me**.
n-j	Jesse James broke out of the **fine jail**.
j-n	He learned Latin by taking **language lessons**.
f-j	He was only **half joking**.

j-f	In her hair she wore **orange feathers**.
v-j	The king forgave the **brave jester**.
j-v	Over the door there grew a **large vine**.
th-j	I always have my breakfast **with juice**.
j-th	I like them so, I will not **change them**.
sh-j	The people on the boat cheered when the **fish jumped**.
j-sh	A jumbo shrimp is a **huge shrimp**.
ch-j	It is hard to **catch jaguars**.
j-ch	Peter Pan is not an **average child**.
j-r	He designs structures to **bridge rivers**.
r-j	We put a lot of fresh fruit in **our jam**.
l-j	Jack was not afraid of the **tall giant**.
j-l	The teacher decided to **change lessons**.
s-j	We all laughed when our **boss joked**.
j-y	My favorite treat is **orange yogurt**.

IMPORTANT CONCEPTS
AND VOCABULARY

The words and ideas below are those that children should master before they enter kindergarten. The games designed and presented in this book introduce and support these concepts in many ways for multiple purposes. In addition to social competence these concepts form the basis for academic success in literacy and math.

Parts of the Body

1. Head
   - Eyes
   - Hair
   - Nose
   - Mouth
     - Teeth
     - Tongue
     - Lips
2. Face
   - Forehead
   - Eyebrows
   - Cheeks

3. Body
   - Arm/Hand/Fingers
   - Belly Button/Tummy
   - Leg/Knee/Thigh
   - Toes/Foot
   - Back
   - Butt
4. Five Senses
   - See (Eyes)
   - Hear (Ears)
   - Feel (Skin)
   - Taste (Tongue)
   - Smell (Nose)

Occupations/People

1. Woman/Mommy	12. Queen
2. Man/Daddy	13. Joker
3. People	14. Knight
4. Teacher	15. Prince
5. Firefighter	16. Princess
6. Doctor	17. Genie
7. Police Officer	18. Fairy
8. Boy/Brother	19. Soldier
9. Girl/Sister	20. Mermaid
10. Baby	21. Clown
11. King	

Places

1. House	12. School
2. Apartment	13. Country
3. Kitchen	14. Beach
4. Bathroom	15. Campsite
5. Bedroom	16. Grocery Store
6. Living Room	17. Doctor's Office
7. Garage	18. Department Store
8. Playground	19. Museum
9. Farm	20. Toy Store
10. Barn	21. Discount Store
11. City	

Food

1. Apples	5. Strawberries
2. Grapes	6. Raspberries
3. Bananas	7. Ice cream
4. Blueberries	8. Ice

9. Cookies
10. Crackers
11. Cheese
12. Ham
13. Bologna
14. Peanut Butter
15. Jelly
16. Bread
17. Mayonnaise
18. Canned Tuna
19. Macaroni
20. Peas

21. Eggs
22. Sandwiches
23. Soup
24. Cereal
25. Pineapples
26. Pretzels
27. Potato Chips
28. Hamburgers
29. Hot Dogs
30. Peppers
31. Carrots
32. Squash

Clothing

1. Raincoat
2. Jacket
3. Pants
4. Shoes
5. Socks
6. Hat

7. Gloves
8. Shirt
9. Dress
10. Diaper
11. Shorts
12. Sweater

Toys

1. Bicycle
2. Puzzle
3. Wooden Blocks
4. Doll

5. Book
6. Ball
7. Wagon
8. Action Figure

Things

1.	Cup	16.	School Bus
2.	Baby Bottle	17.	City Bus
3.	Bowl	18.	Bathtub
4.	Plate	19.	Toilet
5.	Spoon	20.	Towel
6.	Fork	21.	Shampoo
7.	Knife	22.	Soap
8.	Crib	23.	Airplane
9.	Bed	24.	Toothbrush
10.	Pillow	25.	Stove
11.	Blanket	26.	Refrigerator
12.	Phone	27.	Closet
13.	Umbrella	28.	Pots and Pans
14.	Car	29.	Wooden Spoons
15.	Truck		

Plants

1.	Tree	2.	Flower

Pets

1.	Dog	5.	Rabbit
2.	Puppy	6.	Fish
3.	Cat	7.	Hamster
4.	Kitten	8.	Bird

Farm Animals

1. Mouse
2. Cow
   - Calf
3. Horse
   - Foal
4. Sheep
   - Lamb

5. Chicken
   - Chick
   - Egg
6. Rooster
7. Duck
   - Duckling
8. Pig
   - Piglet

Insects

1. Ant
2. Spider
   - Web

3. Bee
   - Hive

Forest

1. Lizard
2. Bluebird
3. Butterfly
   - Caterpillar

4. Fox
5. Wolf
   - Cub

Jungle

1. Snake
2. Elephant

3. Lion
4. Tiger

Water

1. Frog
   - Tadpole
2. Fish
3. Crab

4. Whale
5. Dolphin
6. Octopus

CONCEPTS

Opposites

1. Dark
2. Light
3. Open
4. Closed
5. Empty
6. Full
7. Same
8. Different
9. Front
10. Back/Behind
11. Before
12. After

13. Fast
14. Slow
15. Near
16. Far
17. Wet
18. Dry
19. Hot
20. Cold
21. Inside
22. Outside
23. Good
24. Bad

Texture

1. Rough
   - Bumpy
2. Smooth
3. Hard
4. Soft
   - Fluffy

5. Crunchy
   - Crisp
6. Sweet
7. Salty
8. Sour
9. Juicy

Rhymes

1. Big/Fig
2. Back/Sack
3. Nail/Pail

4. Star/Car
5. Sun/Run

Weather

1. Daytime
2. Nighttime
3. Rain
   - Puddle

4. Snow
   - Snowman
5. Wind
6. Rainbow
   - Colorful

Social

1. Birthday
2. Holiday
3. Fair
4. Share
5. Group

6. First
7. Last
8. Second
9. Third

Possession

1. Mine
2. Yours
3. Ours

4. His
5. Hers
6. Theirs

PRE-ACADEMIC

1. Letters A to Z
2. Numbers/One to One Correspondence/Counting
   - One
   - Two
   - Three
   - Four
   - Five
   - Six
   - Seven
   - Eight
   - Nine
   - Ten
3. Pair
   - Little/Small
   - Big
   - Medium
4. Shapes
   - Line
   - Circle
   - Square
   - Triangle
   - Rectangle
   - Octagon
5. Parts of Speech
   - Verbs
     - Action Verbs
       - Walk
       - Crawl
       - Sleep
       - Dance
       - Play
       - Run
       - Sit

- Blow
- Sing
- Drink
- Eat
- Swing
- Past Tense: ed
- Present Tense: ing
- Third-person Singular: s, es
- Object Verbs
  - Take
  - Push
  - Pull
  - Put
  - Fold
  - Cook
  - Make/Create
  - Clean
  - Paint/Draw

ONLINE RESOURCES

There is a wealth of information available to you at libraries and online. Here are a few suggestions for you to explore.

If you are seeking examples of children telling stories or the interaction between parents and children, there is no better resource than YouTube. These are some of my favorites. Babies' reactions to mushy peas are always entertaining.

"Cute Baby Reaction to Peas - Baby Discovering New Food"
https://www.youtube.com/watch?v=RT675nUEpuk

"No Mashed Peas! Pt. 1"
https://www.youtube.com/watch?v=nBhRUtAL5F0

Here is a YouTube video that went viral. It illustrates the charm of a four-month-old's communication style. Note how the child's reactions inspire his father to respond. Four-month-old genius in action.

"Nash Talking to His Daddy - 4 Months Old"
https://www.youtube.com/watch?v=LsWMyrq3E1U

These YouTube videos show terrific examples of the Parent Skills described in chapter 1 in simultaneous use. Terrific!

"Dad and Son Have Adorable Conversation"
https://www.youtube.com/watch?v=DOfEu2zqrkQ

"Sicilian Discussion with Bisnonna"
https://www.youtube.com/watch?v=tYk6TWFfICI

"3-Year-Old Girl Tells Hilarious Nonsensical Stories"
https://www.youtube.com/watch?v=2M06bwf8mQ0

Here you have a four-year-old telling stories. Notice the growing mastery of narrative. There is a definite story with a series of events, although all grammatic elements are not yet in place. Very little prompting is necessary.

"The Christmas Story (Told By a 4 Year Old)"
https://www.youtube.com/watch?v=Ji0r3ChfVL4

"4 Year Old Telling a Story"
https://www.youtube.com/watch?v=yh1HISTdmH0

Finally, we have eight-year-olds telling stories. Note that at this point the eight-year-old can relate experiences as a comprehensible series of events. With a known tale the eight-year-old is very aware that there is a proper way to tell the story, mimicking the inflections he has heard when an adult told him the story. Grammatic elements such as verb tense are in place.

"8-Year-Old Tornado Survivor Tells Her Story"
https://www.youtube.com/watch?v=liy54O1cSt4

"8 Year Old Tells the Christmas Story"
https://www.youtube.com/watch?v=E-qWtsyoQkM

If you want more information about child development, speech, language, hearing, games, and activities, here are a few of the best online resources:

- American Speech-Language-Hearing Association (ASHA): Making effective communication, a human right, accessible and achievable for all.
  www.asha.org

- *Parents* magazine: An American mass-circulation monthly magazine published by Meredith Corporation that features scientific information on child development geared to help parents in raising their children.
  www.parents.com

- *FamilyFun* magazine: A family magazine published eight times annually by Meredith Corporation, *FamilyFun* is written for parents with children aged three to twelve, and focuses on family cooking, vacations, parties, holidays, crafts, and learning.
  www.parents.com/familyfun-magazine

- Disney Family: A website with Disney-themed crafts and party ideas that are designed to be fun for the whole family.
  https://family.disney.com/crafts/

ILLUSTRATION CREDITS

Megaphone icon by Creative Stall
Arrows icon by Luca Fruzza
Party icon by Hai Studio
Playing cards icon by Georgiana Ionescu
Scissors icon by Baboon Designs
Thought bubble icon by Irene Hoffman
Toy car icon by Tulpahn
Blocks icon by Caesar Rizky Kurniawan

ACKNOWLEDGMENTS

As I write these acknowledgments, it is the middle of March 2020 and the world is in quarantine. I am sending my prayers into the future in the hope that this book finds everyone well, happy, and out of doors enjoying life again. We must learn to take the time to be thankful for so many things as we are all finding out what really matters in life. I am grateful for my family. I want to thank my incredible husband, Noah, for his faith in me, not to mention his professional assistance when my computer was uncooperative. Thanks also to my children (now grown), Joe and Kate, who, along with my "speech room" students, were my guinea pigs as I experimented with language-learning games and activities. I have a special place in my heart for my friends and colleagues: Eileen Misrahi, Craig and Judith Carter, Randy Dashefsky, and Cathy Royse, who acted as a cheering section when I was feeling overwhelmed and patiently let me talk it through. Of course, nothing would have been possible without the highly professional people at Simon & Schuster and Tiller Press. A project like this requires the help and support of many. This book would never have been written without Tiller Cultural Intelligence Analyst Kate Davids, who encouraged me to bring my ideas to the people at Tiller in the first place. I particularly want to say thank you to my patient senior editor, Emily Carleton; the lovely Michael Anderson, Cultural Intelligence Analyst; my diligent editorial assistant, Samantha Lubash; and everyone else at Tiller who worked so hard to bring this book to you. Enjoy!

ABOUT THE AUTHOR

Francine Davids is a retired speech pathologist who worked in the largest elementary school district in Arizona. There, she led the team of speech pathologists working on speech and language evaluations and program development, as well as therapy.